GENDER EQUITY AND AUSTRALIAN IMMIGRATION POLICY

Ruth Fincher
University of Melbourne

Lois Foster
La Trobe University

Rosemary Wilmot
Department of Immigration and Ethnic Affairs
(Victoria)

Australian Government Publishing Service, Canberra

Designed by Helmut Stenzel
Cover design by Helmut Stenzel
Typeset by Abb-typesetting Pty Ltd
Printed for AGPS by Brown Prior Anderson Pty Ltd

Foreword

The Bureau of Immigration and Population Research has already made several contributions to the study of gender issues in immigration. This publication by Ruth Fincher, Lois Foster and Rosemary Wilmot is a notable addition.

Previous initiatives have included the survey by Ros Madden and Susan Young of MSJ Keys Young Planners Ltd entitled *Women and Men Immigrating to Australia: Their Characteristics and Immigration Decisions* (AGPS, Canberra, 1993), and a major conference on Women in Migration, which the Bureau organised at Ormond College, University of Melbourne, in February 1992.

At this conference, the importance of the topic was stressed by Madden and Young:

> Women now make up just over 50 per cent of permanent migration to Australia. But most migration statistics and research ignore the vital gender dimension of the whole immigration process. Few studies to date have systematically explored the particular circumstances of immigrant women or immigrant men, and much research appears to have assumed that the experience is similar regardless of gender. (*BIR Bulletin*, No. 6, April 1992, p. 5).

The secretary of the Department of Immigration and Ethnic Affairs, Mr Chris Conybeare, on the same occasion stressed the significance of the subject:

> It is important because women are now the majority of our immigration intake. How they fare is an issue of social justice. It is also an issue of credibility in a country committed to non-discrimination and effective use of its resources. (*BIR Bulletin*, No. 6, April 1992, p. 5)

Much of the credit for conceiving and bringing to fruition these Bureau contributions to gender in immigration studies belongs to Dr Ruth Fincher and Dr Lois Foster when they were part of the staff of the Bureau, while on leave from their posts at the University of Melbourne and La Trobe University respectively.

With Rosemary Wilmot, Dr Fincher and Dr Foster have now completed this useful study, *Gender Equity and Australian Immigration
Policy.* The work approaches the issue of gender equity in immigation
by reviewing government regulation of gendered flows (chapter 2),
assessing whether there is equity in the relationship between marriage and immigration status (chapter 3), and analysing the influence
of the state on immigrant women's settlement prospects (chapter 4).
It also provides in chapter 5 an overview of immigration, gender
equity and policy.

The study is scholarly and offers several important considerations
for policy-makers. There is much useful information, including the
very interesting insights in chapter 2 to the past reasoning and atti-
tudes of government to gender in determining immigration flows.
The work deserves the wide readership which the Bureau's other
publications on women's issues have received, and which will un-
doubtedly apply also to *Gender Equity and Australian Immigration
Policy.*

JOHN NIEUWENHUYSEN
Director, Bureau of Immigration and Population Research

Contents

List of figures and tables

Figures

Tables

The authors

Ruth Fincher is Senior Lecturer in Geography at the University of Melbourne. She returned to Australia from North America in 1985, after twelve years away completing a PhD and teaching in universities there. Her research interests include gender, class and ethnic relations in metropolitan environments, and theories of the state and social justice. Recent publications include *Immigration, Urban Infrastructure and the Environment* (1991) and articles on representations of women in Australian urban and social policies.

Lois Foster is a Reader in Sociology within the Graduate School of Education at La Trobe University. She holds a PhD from the University of Alberta, Canada. Her research interests are in the sociology of immigration, ethnic relations, education and women. Most recently, she has contributed to an extensive comparative analysis of Australian and Canadian immigration and refugee policy funded by the Bureau of Immigration and Population Research and Employment and Immigration Canada.

Rosemary Wilmot has worked in operational sections of the Department of Immigration and Ethnic Affairs since 1988. She has a BA(Hons) from the University of Melbourne and majored in Political Science and Chinese.

Acknowledgments

This monograph began its long journey to final publication in 1991, when two of us (Ruth Fincher and Lois Foster) were working for a couple of years in the Bureau of Immigration Research (as it was then). Though one of us (Lois) was there primarily because of her capacities in sociology and education, and the other (Ruth) for her interests in urban and environmental issues, we found we had a concern in common with gender relations, especially the ways these affected women, in the context of migration to Australia.

So we set out to express our understanding of the importance of gender issues in analyses of immigration through the organisation of three activities within the Bureau: the commissioning of a major data assembling and gathering consultancy on the characteristics and decision-making of men and women migrating to Australia (Madden & Young 1993b); the sponsoring of a national conference on Women in Migration (which was held in Melbourne in February 1992); and the writing of a review monograph (by us) which would draw together Australian literature and policy material that was relevant to any assessment of the gendered nature of immigration policy, but which had not been assembled in such a way before.

The third of us (Rosemary Wilmot) joined the Bureau to work on the review project, using her particular expertise as a researcher but also as a member of the DILGEA operational staff. This piece of work has taken a long time to come to fruition because we all left the Bureau before the manuscript had been even nearly completed, to return to our places of prior employment.

Our first thanks, then, are to those at the Bureau who have been willing to wait such a long time for the manuscript, agreeing with us over the importance of its topic. Dr John Nieuwenhuysen (BIPR Director) and Dr Lynne Williams (BIPR Assistant Director) have our particular gratitude here. Ms Vicki Thompson, also at the Bureau, has been an absolutely major support to us, willingly keying in our numerous revisions to the manuscript, always cheerfully, pleasantly and with great skill.

At the project's very beginning, Anne Seitz of Swinburne University of Technology and Srebrenka Kunek of Monash University provided useful suggestions, as did Ann Smith of the Department of Immigration and Ethnic Affairs in Canberra. We greatly appreciated their insights. Jacqueline Coleman, BIPR Librarian in Melbourne, and Michelle Bilobrk, of Archives in DIEA in Canberra, were extremely helpful in obtaining for us copies of large numbers of files, books and reports. The work could not have been written without their very considerable skills and assistance, and we thank them for this. (And how will we ever forget going to the DIEA Archives in Canberra searching without success for material under the subject heading 'Women', only to find the files we wanted under the heading 'Females', preceded by the subject headings 'Fascists' and 'Fauna'!)

Later on we interviewed many immigration officers about their experiences in overseas postings. We are very grateful for the time they gave us and the frankness with which they spoke to us. We also interviewed numerous women who themselves were immigrants and have become activists in Australia, working in the interests of women (in particular) in their communities. We thank them most sincerely for the time they gave us and for their willingness to discuss their work fully and openly.

The manuscript has been through many revisions. In the course of these, Dr Lynne Williams was a great help in ensuring that the labour force material was quite accurate and up to date. And the two external referees who read a very long early draft were of enormous assistance to us in suggesting more appropriate foci and where the manuscript should be pruned or extended. Our thanks indeed to these women.

Abbreviations

AAT	Administrative Appeals Tribunal
ABS	Australian Bureau of Statistics
ADJR	Administrative Decisions (Judicial Review)
ALP	Australian Labor Party
AMEP	Adult Migrant Education Program
AMES	Adult Migrant Education Service
ANESBWA	Association of Non-English Speaking Background Women of Australia
ASCO	Australian Standard Classification of Occupations
BIPR	Bureau of Immigration and Population Research, formerly the BIR
BIR	Bureau of Immigration Research
CES	Commonwealth Employment Service
CMO	Chief Migration Officer
CURA	Centre for Urban Research and Action
DEET	Department of Employment, Education and Training
DIEA	Department of Immigration and Ethnic Affairs
DILGEA	Department of Immigration, Local Government and Ethnic Affairs
DSS	Department of Social Security
ESB	English-speaking background
FOI	Freedom of Information

IRT	Immigration Review Tribunal
JSCMR	Joint Standing Committee on Migration Regulations
NESB	Non-English-speaking background
NOOSR	National Office of Overseas Skill Recognition
NUMAS	Numerical Assessment System
OECD	Organisation for Economic Co-operation and Development
PES	Professional Employment Service
PSC	Public Service Commission
TAFE	Technical and Further Education
UK	United Kingdom

Executive summary

Migration flows are made up of men and women, not just of people—migration flows are gendered, and there are reasons why they have the gender characteristics they do. To understand not only why and in what ways gender is a factor in intra- and inter-country movements of people, but also how government policies have intended and unintended gendered effects in migration and settlement, is a central aim of migration studies. Paradoxically, the literature on this topic is relatively sparse. For these reasons, the present study on gender and Australian immigration policy seeks to illuminate processes and relationships about which little is known.

The study assesses Australian immigration policy against two criteria of gender equity or gender justice drawn from recent feminist writings. The criteria are:

❑ the degree to which the policies take seriously the identified differences of their constituents, including those of gender;

❑ the degree to which the voices of disadvantaged social groups are sought, heard and taken into account in the policy-making process.

With these criteria in mind, questions are posed in the study about how women and men fare under particular policy regimes, and whether certain expectations about men and women, masculinity and femininity, result in disadvantage for those who do not comply with or fit the expected models. The gender justice approach taken in the study seeks to identify apparent biases in the definitions and practices used in the policies discussed. One firm implication of such an analysis is that the disadvantage or advantage experienced by immigrants to Australia is institutionally constructed and not derived from the personal qualities of immigrants.

As a consequence of examining from a gender equity viewpoint the nature and consequences of state intervention in immigration and settlement, the study offers some suggestions for the modification of official policy towards immigrants, and more especially towards women.

Chapter 2 examines government regulation of gendered immigration flows, documenting the ways that immigration selection in the period after the Second World War has represented male and (particularly) female immigrants in ways that, currently, are seen as inaccurate and inequitable. The assessment is made on the grounds that selection has been based on definitions and understandings of skill that are gender-biased or on the expectation that women will enter Australia as dependent family members. The data analysed include immigration policies, official handbooks issued to immigration officers in overseas posts, responses by selected immigration officers to face-to-face interviews and a comparison of views on gender expressed by the Department of Immigration and the Department of Employment, Education and Training.

In chapter 3, the close links between marital status and immigration status and the state's role in tightening those links for many women migrating to Australia as permanent settlers are explored. This is done by analysing legal definitions of marriage currently used by the Australian state in the selection of immigrants, statistical data on numbers of immigrants entering by virtue of their marital status, and marriage-related scenarios in which the reliance on marital status by immigrant women is revealed. It is suggested that the marriage–immigration tie disadvantages potential or actual immigrant women with respect to skills recognition, vulnerability in change of status and sham marriage situations. In that marital status is a more important factor for women than men and that there may be gender inequities in immigration flowing from this, then the marriage–immigration tie is influenced by the deliberate actions of the state and becomes a public concern.

Settlement issues rather than immigration processes are the focus of chapter 4. The study concludes that many immigrant women have been disadvantaged as an indirect product of immigration policies by the extended paid labour force commitments and family duties that they have had to assume. The consequent 'double burden' they have suffered arose because of the precise locations in which employment was available at the times when the Australian Government was admitting large numbers of immigrants, and the failure to provide adequate services of special importance to women in those locations. These were expensive places to live, often requiring two salaries from immigrant households. The statistical and qualitative data examined here describe labour market participation and indirect locational effects, political participation of immigrant women and the spatial incidence of settlement services especially important for women, such as child care and language services.

In chapter 5, a summary of the major findings of the study is provided and discussed, having taken into account the gender equity criteria, under three headings: 'Allowing for diversity and difference in policy prescriptions', 'Encouraging equitable processes' and 'Gender equity requires continued scrutiny'. The authors suggest that immigration policies and practices can still be improved in the levels of gender equity they achieve for potential immigrants and for settlers already arrived.

Considering whether contemporary immigration policy allows for difference and diversity, the study concludes that masculinist definitions of skill continue to direct certain immigration selection judgments and that this poses difficulties for women applicants. The disproportionate entry of women under rules stipulating that they must be in marital relationships with men is a further issue of gender equity. More precisely for policy, the study questions whether adult members of an immigrant household should be designated Principal Applicant or not, when the person (usually a male) designated as such receives better treatment with regard to skills recognition than the other members of the household. These are issues of policy outcome.

With regard to whether immigration policy operates with equitable processes, the study suggests better processes for informing prospective women immigrants of their likely circumstances in Australia. It also raises the possibility of an enhanced role for the settlement agencies of the Australian state, to extend their role in advocating respect for difference among the many institutions and organisations that affect settlement prospects.

Continued conceptual scrutiny of immigration policy is necessary, of course, to ensure that new understandings are conveyed about what constitutes the privileging of masculinity and femininity in certain forms that may be undesirable. The study flags the link between marriage and immigration as of concern here. Equally obviously, there are many ways in which the actual practice of immigration and settlement procedures requires alteration, when it becomes clear that certain groups of men or women may be disadvantaged by it.

Chapter 1: Gender equity and the analysis of immigration and settlement

Immigration has been a topic of particular interest for many disciplines, including demography, economics, geography, political science and sociology. In spite of this, when one attempts to identify a literature dealing with gender in immigration, and specifically women and immigration, the pool of resources is considerably circumscribed. Much more attention has been given to Third World women's migration (intra-country and between Third World countries, or guestworker migration from Third to First World countries) and the phenomenon of female refugee movements and experiences, than to women's immigration to the countries of recognised permanent immigration, that is, Australia, Canada, New Zealand and the United States.

The focus of this study is gender equity in Australian immigration policy as it applies to the immigrant selection process and the experience of settlement. So, we will ask questions about how women and men fare under particular policy regimes, and whether certain expectations about men and women, masculinity and femininity, result in disadvantage for those who do not comply with or fit the expected models. We will be making efforts to identify ways that immigration and settlement policies seem to have been just or unjust in gender terms.

Gender equity in contemporary feminist thought

In taking up a concern here with issues of gender equity, some of the ideas of particular feminist theorists of gender justice are being followed and directed to the policy contexts of immigration and settlement. These thinkers are grappling with the thorny issue of how to establish policies and processes that are just for all involved, while viewing differences between social groups, like gender, as indicating specificity and heterogeneity rather than otherness and opposition. Other important points from this literature follow.

1

First, institutions and institutional players are significant in producing outcomes and processes that are more or less just. The point is
often made that avowedly gender-neutral or gender-blind policies are
rarely neutral in their effects on disadvantaged groups, often cement-
ing the social and economic position of vulnerable individuals (Jaggar
1991, p. 96 and see Young 1990, p. 169). Value judgments are em-
bedded in administrative practices that are apparently innocent: this
has led to a denial by some authors of the possibility of impartiality
and the claim that disadvantaged groups must be sought out by
specific administrative mechanisms so that their cases are heard
(Young 1990). An extension of this argument is that the merit principle on which much policy selection (including immigration policy
selection of immigrants based on skills measures) is based is quite
flawed, because merit is impossible to measure and because the
ranking of qualifications and skills is fundamentally political rather
than impartial (Young 1990).

Secondly, there is of course a difficulty in naming social groups
that do not comply with or gain from orthodox and supposedly
neutral policy procedures. Nominating categories of disadvantage,
such as women or particular language groups, not only imposes false
homogeneity on people who might be administratively assigned to
those groups, but also may stigmatise people choosing to align themselves to such designations if they are then seen as other than the
norm. As Pettman (1992, p. 2) has so usefully stated in her analysis of
the imposition of categories on people in Australia, ethnic-minority
women have in many ways (policy and other) been 'contained
within the "normalised absence/pathologised presence" couplet',
their inclusion for special attention in policy and conceptual thinking depending on their 'differences' being seen as 'other' and
'opposition'.

Selective stigmatisation of social groups would not be just. Does
this mean that all categories should be suspended? No, for that would
mean that the task of policy-making for progressive change is not
possible, and that political mobilisation on the basis of preferred categories would be impossible too. It does require recognition, however,
that categories are interpretations made for certain purposes—even
apparently obvious categories like 'immigrant'. Taking this example, to
illustrate and following Pettman (1992, p. 52), when does an immigrant cease to be an immigrant? Is it after several generations? This
can be posed as an administrative problem, and will be defined for
administratively political reasons (as with 'settlement' being viewed
administratively and financially as not taking longer than 2–3 years)
with implications for justice and equity. But then certain people may
designate themselves as 'migrant' even if born in a location of
migrant destination—because it is a designation that joins them to a
social group with which they feel affinity. The implication is that
categories are more acceptably or justly used if they represent groups
of affinity formed by people who wish to be so designated, and who

use them to maintain and claim their difference, than if they are imposed without consultation as tools of bureaucratic management.

Thirdly, analysts identify the significance for women of the way they are incorporated into the paid labour force, as something which affects all other aspects of their lives. Chafetz (1990), for example, argues for the primacy of the gender division of labour in the analysis of gender equity, claiming that women's economic dependency on men is a major sustainer of gender inequity, and that if women gain greater access to resource generation (usually through paid work) then this is often associated with reductions in the 'levels' of gender inequality. A more subtle and historically situated position is presented by Pettman (1992, p. 45), who notes that the *modes* (not just the fact) of incorporation of Australian immigrant women into the paid labour force 'load their choices and opportunities in almost every area of their lives'.

Clearly in this interpretation, paid work force participation can be advantageous or not, depending on a range of factors, including how it compares with a person's previous circumstances, or precisely how it affects other aspects of their lives. A point we have taken up, then, is that opportunities for resource generation are very significant for gender justice, though crude measures like levels of work force participation do not indicate whether greater justice or injustice for immigrant women results.

Criteria of gender justice against which policy outcomes and processes leading to them can be examined, then, include:

☐ the degree to which policies take seriously the identified differences of their constituents, including those of gender, and make amends for the disadvantage associated with some of those differences (in a way that does not require elimination of the differences);

☐ the degree to which the voices of disadvantaged social groups, formed by affinity rather than by bureaucratic categorisation, are sought, heard and taken into account in the policy-making process.

Concern with these issues is threaded through the following chapters and drawn together in chapter 5.

The gender justice approach we are taking is to identify what appear to be biases in the definitions and practices used in the policies discussed. In situating women to the fore in our discussion of immigration policies in Australia we are trying to identify some ways in which their disadvantage (or advantage if it happens) is institutionally constructed.

Gender—a valid perspective on migration?

Why should gender be a matter for inclusion in analyses of migration? Why treat immigrants as men or women, rather than as

3

'people' or 'individuals'? Why consider immigrant women as a group or set of groups comprising people of somewhat similar circumstances, so differentiating them from immigrant men as a group or set of groups? Indeed, a claim was made in 1976 by Anthony Leeds that 'women' is not an appropriate category for analysis in studies of migration, being a rhetorical or ideological term and not a scientific one. Rather than looking at individuals (e.g. women), claimed Leeds, we should look at collectivities in the migration process to discover how and why people migrate.

Since that time, considerable research has shown how migration is a thoroughly gendered process—that people take part in it as members of particular groups (families, communities, class and ethnic groups) but also that their migration and experience in destinations or places of settlement are influenced by the gender, class and race relations of the collectivities in which they come to live. Further, it is clear that a focus on gender as an important dimension of the migration process does not involve separating out individuals who are 'male' or 'female' from the broader contexts in which they live their lives, or from other aspects of social diversity like class and life course stage.

A focus on gender relations in immigration should redress the lack of attention paid to the specific circumstances of women migrating, in all their complexity. And it might avoid the tendency of some literature to depict women immigrants merely as problematic deviants from the male migrant 'norm'. Authors who argue strongly for a rigorous focus on gender issues in migration, for these reasons, are Smith (1980), Wellesley Editorial Committee (1977) and Martin (1991); Morokvasic (1983) has noted several stages through which international research on women in migration has passed since the 1970s (though research and policies based on some of the earlier thinking persist). It is clear from her chronology that, as time has passed, some failures of the migration literature to consider gender issues and women, or to do this in unacceptable, stereotypical ways, have been rectified.

Apart from the theoretical reasons for considering gender relations as integral to the migration process and experiences of it, there have been a range of empirical reasons proposed for a major focus on women migrating and for disaggregation of the information about migration by sex. In the Australian case, for example, a focus on women seems demanded by the fact that more women have recently migrated to Australia than men, and women comprise almost 50 per cent of the flow of temporary migrants to Australia (Madden & Young 1993b). Internationally, growing attention is being paid to the numbers of men and women involved in different aspects of the migration and settlement process. Women and men, for example, fill different niches in industries and occupations in countries of settlement (Fawcett, Khoo & Smith 1984, p. 4). In some places, a transition has been observed from males being immigrant pioneers, to females taking up this role (Cohen 1977, p. 27).

Of course, not every part of the vast international literature on migration is germane to our commentary on gender equity in Australia's recent immigration history, even if much of that literature is gender blind. The international migration literature reports on internal migration within different countries and continents, and international migration between First World and Third World countries, between different First World countries, and so on. It also analyses the migration of people (women and men) bearing different types of immigration status. Guest workers, contract or indentured labourers, permanent settlers who may be refugees, economic immigrants or settlers migrating under family reunion provisions—all these migrants are included in the literature. As has been pointed out in a most insightful paper, it is necessary to distinguish different types of migration streams, in terms of their direction and the status of their participants (Gibson & Graham 1986).

Accordingly, in this monograph we will draw on that literature from the international offerings which seems to provide the most useful comparison with the recent Australian situation. That is, we will select for review only that literature analysing international (rather than internal) migration, flows to First World countries, and permanent settler immigration. We will not consider, except in passing, the special circumstances of refugees, as they are a relatively small group in Australia's immigrant intake. And, of course, we will include in our purposive review only that literature that differentiates women and men, and that focuses on women alone. These limits to the extent of the review in this study are not intended to suggest that topics excluded are less worthy of study: for example, the particular hardships of women refugees, and the difference it makes if one is a 'temporary' migrant (like a guest worker, or an indentured labourer) without full citizenship in one's destination, are important avenues for others to pursue.

Applying a gender-equity framework to immigration and settlement in Australia

In this monograph we are seeking to determine whether there are ways in which processes structuring immigration and settlement are in fact gendered processes, and result in different outcomes for immigrant men and women in Australia. The processes of concern to us are practices of the Australian state, generally speaking the Immigration Department.[1]

The study, as we have said, is limited to considering settler arrivals, and within this group its focus is on economic and family immigrants rather than refugees. Accordingly, its first concern is to examine the practices of the Australian state in selecting permanent settlers for entry as economic or family reunion immigrants. Consistent with the gender equity criteria identified already, attention will be paid to the actual processes or routine practices through which selection of immigrants for Australia occurs, and the relative advantages and disadvantages incurred by men and women therein. This means we are asking not only how the selection procedures might affect the subsequent settlement prospects of immigrants once in Australia, but also how well and how accurately prospective male and (particularly) female immigrants are represented in government decision-making about choice of immigrants.

The examination of immigrant selection by the Australian state occurs in chapter 2. Pertinent literature from countries other than Australia testifies to the importance for immigrant women of the precise institutional policies and practices of governments (and indeed other 'gatekeeping' bodies) regulating their emigration and immigration. The central section of the chapter is a presentation of the gendered nature of immigrant selection in Australia since the Second World War, drawing on evidence from Immigration Department files, selection manuals for overseas officers, and interviews with immigration officers who have been based overseas.

The 'containment' of women in immigration categories associated with 'family reunion' rather than 'skill' is argued to be one outcome of the gendered processes of immigrant selection described. The focus on selection of immigrants and its implications for immigrant women continues in chapter 3, which takes up the issue of the strong link between immigrant women's marital status and their immigration status. It is a development of the material in chapter 2, in that it looks at one way in which the rules of entry to Australia envisage women in certain guises (as married, or fiancées, and certainly in relation to men), and therefore encourage women to comply with this image (perhaps not always as they would have wanted) in order to enter Australia.

The chapter asks the question: How does marital status shape people's experience of immigration and how equitable is this in gender terms? Some general circumstances are identified in which marital status appears to be directly linked to immigration. They include:

❏ people entering as would be 'normally' envisaged under the preferential family category (wives joining husbands or vice versa);

❏ Australian residents travelling overseas (often to their place of birth) to find a husband or wife;

❏ illegal sham marriages.

Specific implications for women of these links between marriage and immigration to Australia, in each of the scenarios described, are given, alongside comments about the gender equity involved in tying immigration to marital status so tightly.

Moving to consider the settlement experiences of immigrants, women in particular, raises any number of queries about levels of gender equity. How immigrants have fared in Australia, once having migrated in the post-Second World War decades, has been examined in a considerable literature concerning their occupations, industries, their success in particular labour markets, their access to services and to a range of other opportunities. Rarely are the relative circumstances of immigrant men and women compared in this literature, however. Sometimes their circumstances are compared with those of the Australia-born—this occurs, especially, in labour force statistics. There are different ways in which gender equity associated with international migration might be considered. On the one hand, people's circumstances before and after migration might be compared, with a claim made that the migration and settlement process had been equitable if the circumstances before and after migration remained similar, or had not deteriorated. On the other hand, men's and women's circumstances after settlement, in the place of destination, might be compared, with the claim being made that if their circumstances were similar, or they were experiencing a similar level of 'advantage' or 'disadvantage', then gender equity prevailed. We have chosen to develop our judgments by comparing men's and women's circumstances in the country of destination. This is itself difficult—for one would not want to imply that women and men had to be the same in order to be equal—that old feminist dilemma. We have chosen this approach because it is a track less fraught than that of trying to evaluate people's circumstances before and after migration (as Tienda and Booth (1991) certainly demonstrate).

Accordingly, chapter 4 marshals evidence about forms of participation by immigrant women in an important aspect of their 'settlement' in Australia (the world of paid work) and makes claims about how this differs from the circumstances of immigrant men. The 'settlement process', of which such participation is an outcome, is of course partly structured by the practices of the state. A central question about gender equity posed by chapter 4, then, having noted levels and forms of women's participation in the work force, is what have been the effects on this 'settlement process' of the immigration selection emphasis on women as 'dependants' who were 'less skilled' than male immigrants? More broadly, how is the settlement process gendered, and how is such gendering related to state practices and policies?

We conclude that the state's immigration policies have affected women's encounters with the paid work force indirectly. Since the Second World War, immigrants have located themselves primarily in metropolitan areas, because of the employment opportunities available there at the time the immigrant intake was large, and subsequently also because of the presence of family and friends in such locations. These labour and housing markets were, therefore, indirectly 'selected' for immigrants by the state because of the work those immigrants were brought to Australia to do. Finding themselves in places where the cost of living was relatively high, immigrant women entered the paid work force, full time, in large numbers, while continuing as well the domestic labour of their households. This 'double burden' of paid and unpaid work, the former often limited to arduous, low-paid employment, is the indirect legacy for many immigrant women of the context in which immigration policy operated in Australia. This burden has been accentuated for many women from non-English-speaking-background (NESB) countries, when their language and cultural attributes have been the subject of stigmatisation and even discrimination in the Australian context.

It is very clear that there are a host of institutions and situations other than government that affect the prospects of immigrants to Australia, once here at their destination. Gender equity for immigrants settling is more than just a government concern. Nevertheless, there are points that can be made about the way the state interacts with non-government institutions, seeking to improve the forms of participation of immigrant women in aspects of Australian life. We develop points such as this in the concluding chapter, in which some policy implications of our gender equity framework, and our findings, are described.

Chapter 2: Government regulation of gendered immigration flows

The way in which a suitable 'immigrant' is depicted by Australian government policy guidelines has situated women at various times under terms like 'immigrant wives', 'breeders for Australia' and 'unskilled dependants'. Women have been defined in policy and constrained in their movements by their marital status and familial relationships. But women do immigrate, however immigration policy portrays them, and in recent times women have accessed the immigration program and entered Australia through those very social and familial characteristics which had hitherto defined and confined them.

This chapter asks the question: How do government policies and actions help to create an immigrant flow with particular gender characteristics? It is argued that there have been ways of thinking about men and women immigrants and refugees, about what their roles and characteristics should be, that have underpinned immigrant selection in the past four decades. These perceptions have at times led to what we can now identify as inequitable and inaccurate treatment of settlers, both male and female, in the Australian context. The major task of this chapter is to outline the role of the immigration-related policies, personnel and apparatus of the Australian state and to examine their gender implications.

Of course, the issue of the implications for immigrant women and men of the precise governmental framework that regulates their immigration and emigration, has been of concern in countries other than Australia. Sometimes there is a complex mesh of private agencies (either commercial, or charity-based) acting together with government bodies to facilitate the migration of particular (often particularly gendered) people. The Philippines Government of the early 1980s has been noted for its determined efforts to arrange with the governments of other countries a supply of docile, well-trained labourers (male emigrants from the Philippines) to staff construction projects overseas and to send remittances back to the Philippines

(Gibson & Graham 1986, p. 142; Lycklama 1989). And in the late 1980s and early 1990s, Filipino housemaids are being recruited for domestic service in Asian countries such as Hong Kong and Singapore, and also in countries of the Middle East such as Kuwait. In this chapter the recent history of the policies and practices of Australia's governmental immigration bureaucracy will be examined, identifying its expectations of what male and female immigrants would be. There will not be any study of the full range of intermediary organisations through which flows of immigrants are engineered, only one of which is the Australian state. Such study would be valuable, however, and it is clear from just citing the Philippines case, how many implications there would be for gender equity in the manner of interaction between governments and intermediary bodies. As Lycklama (1989, p. 49) argues in her discussion of labour-exporting countries: 'there exists an urgent need to research and analyse the mechanisms through which the respective state bureaucracies are in a possibly more or less close co-operation with such intermediating agencies as recruitment agencies, travel agencies, hotels, banks etc ...'. (Profit-making intermediaries are, however, a different matter altogether from the many voluntary or community-based organisations which work with governments most positively to ease the processes of migration and settlement for immigrants.)

To examine the role of the Department of Immigration as immigration gatekeeper or regulator, we have drawn on a range of sources. These include archival material containing policy statements and rationales; instructions to officers in overseas posts, which contain actual directives on selection criteria; interviews with selected officers to gather information on how they implemented these directives and how they 'constructed' their image of a suitable immigrant; the Immigration Department's oral history on immigration officers; and transcripts from group interviews with immigrants that were part of a consultancy report on women's and men's experiences in the migration process (Madden & Young 1993a). The Corporate and Women's Issues Plans of the Department of Immigration constitute another 'official' view. Finally, there are interpretations of policy produced by commentators such as are to be found in the academic literature.

The entry of legal immigrants to Australia is controlled by the Australian Government through established immigration policy and associated regulations. Implementation of the policy is carried out by the federal Department of Immigration. Immigration selection is the province of the immigration officers located in the overseas posts. Each of these structures serves a gatekeeping purpose; the function and role of gatekeeper, however, is attributed most directly to the immigration officer (though officers' discretion has been reduced in recent decades, as will be clear later in the chapter).

The chapter will include, as background material, an historical overview of immigration policies, and a statistical profile of immigrant numbers, by gender. It will proceed, then, to its major section in which recent immigrant selection policies are reviewed, to identify the representations of men and women they contained and to comment on the gender justice of these. Finally, to emphasise how these gender issues fitted in with contemporary views, there is a brief comparison of the way gender issues were treated within the immigration bureaucracy with the manner of their treatment within another major federal government department, the Department of Employment. Introducing this last section of the chapter raises an interesting broader question which must be alluded to before proceeding.

It is very difficult to make judgments about the past. It is recognised and acknowledged that policies (about immigration, as other matters) are crafted within prevailing discourses, and that judging them from the standpoint of a different current policy discourse and social or gender consciousness is inappropriate. Later in this chapter, accordingly, the stands of immigration policies and practices in the past on gender matters have been assessed, by comparing them with evidence about what the Department of Employment was doing and saying about gender at those same times. This is a very brief and limited attempt to situate the Immigration Department historically; to do the issue full justice would require scrutiny of all the discourses and power relations in which the relevant bureaucrats were participating, including an assessment of the intentions behind certain policies and practices as well as their effects. It would also demand an attempt to situate individual bureaucrats, or groups of them, within the bureaucracy, as to their perceptions, consciousness and use of particular discourses. Little hint of this fascinating history is found in the rest of chapter 2; perhaps such a detailed historical account will appear in a soon-to-be-completed doctoral thesis by Srebrenka Kunek (see also her paper, Kunek 1989).

Overview of immigration policy

What have statements of Australia's immigration policy to tell us about the state's perception of women in the immigration process? Are women *per se* named in such statements? Do the policy statements and any references to gender, or to women specifically, change over time? To find the answers to these questions, policy statements and the handbooks issued by the Immigration Department under successive administrations were consulted. An overview and a brief suggestion of the way women were included in these documents are presented succinctly by means of a table and time-line. Table 2.1 was constructed to represent gendered administrative and policy changes over time and to link them to the particular governments with

Table 2.1: Time-line for immigration selection policy

Date	Federal Government	Administrative changes	General policy	Gendered policy provisions
1949	**Liberal** *Menzies* [Downer]	Discretionary decision-making	Focus on physical attributes	Married women only to migrate with husbands.
1959				
1960				Age for single women 18–35, men 18–45. Fiancées open entry, fiancés bonded.
1961				
1962				
1963	[Opperman]			
1964				No assistance for over 55s with dependants. Prefer trade qualifications. No literacy test for women and minors. No de factos except with joint children. Size.
1965	[Snedden]			
1966	*Holt*			
1967	*McEwen*			
1968	*Gorton*			
1969	[Lynch] [Forbes]	First points assessment		
1971	*McMahon*	Numerical assessment (NUMAS)		Proxy wives accepted.
1972–75	**Australian Labor Party** *Whitlam* [Grassby]		Skill emphasised	Marriageability re-emphasised for women. Unmarried women must be self-reliant. Single parents find own accommodation. Wives' earnings discounted.
1975	**Liberal** *Fraser* [McKellar]			
1976		*Ombudsman Act* *AD(JR) Act*	Family reunion component	Maintenance guarantee. Single M/F 18–45. Any worker literacy-tested.

Year	Party / Minister	Legislation	Notes
1977			
1978			
1979	[Macphee]		Gendered language deleted.
1980			
1981			
1982	[Hodges]	*Freedom of Information Act*	De facto spouses okay. Points for employment and settlement factors.
1983–85	**Australian Labor Party** *Hawke* [West] [Hurford]	Para 6A added to *Migration Act 58*	
1986	[Young]		Increased economic emphasis and decrease in immigration numbers, especially of skill migration. Points for occupation and family factors.
1987	[Holding]		
1988			
1989	[Ray]	Migration Regulations	
1990	[Hand]		
1991	*Keating*		
1992			
1993	[Bolkus]		Points for skill and family factors.

Key: **Party in government** *Prime Minister* [Minister for Immigration]

13

responsibility for immigration at various times in the post-Second World War period.

This time-line is useful to indicate that even though governments may view their immigration policies as gender-neutral, careful examination reveals clear evidence of set views about men's and women's attributes and roles. For example, policies have affirmed immigrant attributes in such a way that certain characteristics rather than others have heightened the probability of selection of women rather than men (and for others, the reverse has operated). There are very particular implications for gender equity in these policy prescriptions. A more extensive analysis of the politics of gender definitions in immigration policy over the past four decades, official documents outlining selection matters, and examples of policy guidelines to be found in the Policy Advice Manuals produced by the Immigration Department after the implementation of the 1989 immigration policy legislation, are found later in the chapter.

The material in table 2.1 is more than a mere chronology; it is a record of significant policy changes resting on definite, even though undeclared, ideological assumptions. As was noted earlier, it is not within the scope of this monograph to analyse why certain shifts occurred in the history of policy-making with regard to immigration. But it is clear from this simple time-line that profound changes did occur.

For example, in 1973 the Labor Government removed the 'White Australia Policy'. This was a bold step, given white Australia's long history of racist exclusion and of discriminatory treatment of residents other than Caucasians (such as Aborigines, Chinese and Torres Strait Islanders). The Whitlam Government, however, needed to exemplify its reformist orientation and to break with the conservatism of the past.

Another instance was the move in 1976 by the Liberal–National Country Party Coalition Government to introduce a new policy whereby: 'The welfare and settlement prospects of the individual migrant will take priority over the immediate needs of the employment market' (Department of Immigration file 76/76327). By this strategy, the Coalition Government identified immigration objectives as 'taking immigration out of the narrow manpower policies which at present dominate it' and emphasised, as an entry criterion, the 'ability to become integrated' to ensure a 'socially cohesive society'. Accordingly, a new system was developed for assessing applicants on a numerical scale which allocated points for age, employment demand and 'financial adequacy of family' in order to assess 'economic viability'. Other elements to be taken into consideration dealt with factors which it was thought identified an applicant's 'willingness and ability to become integrated into Australian society', such as expectations, stability, self-sufficiency, initiative, presentation, knowledge of English, and whether they had been nominated.

Numerical assessment (NUMAS) was adopted in 1978 and introduced a new method of selecting immigrants for Australia. Progressively the factors to which points are allocated have narrowed and in 1992, under a Labor Government, points assessment came to relate only to labour force participation characteristics.

Over the same period, grounds for entry into Australia have become more delineated so that Refugee and Preferential Family categories are not points-assessed, as they have no labour force expectations attached to them. Since December 1989, the Independent category has assessed the age, educational qualifications and English speaking ability of the Principal Applicant. The Concessional Family category replaces English speaking ability with several criteria relating to the relationship, citizenship and settlement of the family sponsor. The growth in the Family categories, that is, the Preferential and Concessional categories, can be interpreted as benefiting women wanting to immigrate to Australia. This is evident as more women meet the eligibility requirements of those categories than of the Skill categories or the Humanitarian categories and more women migrate under Family programs than do men.

Accompanying policy changes are administrative changes. The story revealed in table 2.1 is one which sketches a definite linear reduction of the degree to which gatekeepers, the Immigration Department and its officers, can exercise their discretion. While at one time they were sole arbiters of a person's eligibility to immigrate, the introduction, and increased sophistication, of a points assessment set out the criteria in supposedly objective and clear-cut terms reflected in an unambiguous numerical weighting. At the same time, the introduction of administrative law, including the *Administrative Appeals Tribunal Act 1975*, the *Ombudsman Act 1976*, the *Administrative Decisions (Judicial Review) Act 1977* and the *Freedom of Information Act 1982*, has made gatekeepers more accountable, thereby restricting their discretionary powers. Finally, the revision of the *Migration Act 1958* and the introduction of Migration Regulations in 1989 have further reduced gatekeepers' discretion by describing and defining criteria in greater detail and setting eligibility in law.

In general policy terms, it could be said that Australia's immigration needs have shifted with the changes to Australia's economic and political environment. There had for many decades been governmental clamouring for a larger population for Australia, primarily for defence reasons. Immigration, and women immigrants, could clearly contribute here (see de Lepervanche 1989). A demand for labour in the first three decades of the post-Second World War period also saw a focus on physical attributes which slowly gave way to a greater emphasis on skills and trades as the economy relied more on technical and manufacturing industries. Family reunion became a specified policy on the Liberal Party coming to office in 1975, and was part of their election platform.

15

The summary presented in the table provides initial clues to the gendered nature of immigration policy, flagging matters which are discussed in greater detail in a later section. For example, the size or height requirement as found in the 1964 manual was a criterion before 1964. And maintenance guarantees were included in the 1976 manual as a requirement for sponsors bringing out their wives and children. Such guarantees have existed in one form or another ever since and are more generally applied. The policy provisions listed are taken from the 1959, 1964, 1971, 1972, 1976, 1982 and 1989 manuals. They do not indicate, however, whether those policies were previously introduced by policy circular or later amended by policy circular.

The brief review noted above indicates that immigration policy and the actual program (categories, numbers and composition) are not

Figure 2.1: Immigration program management structure, 1990–91

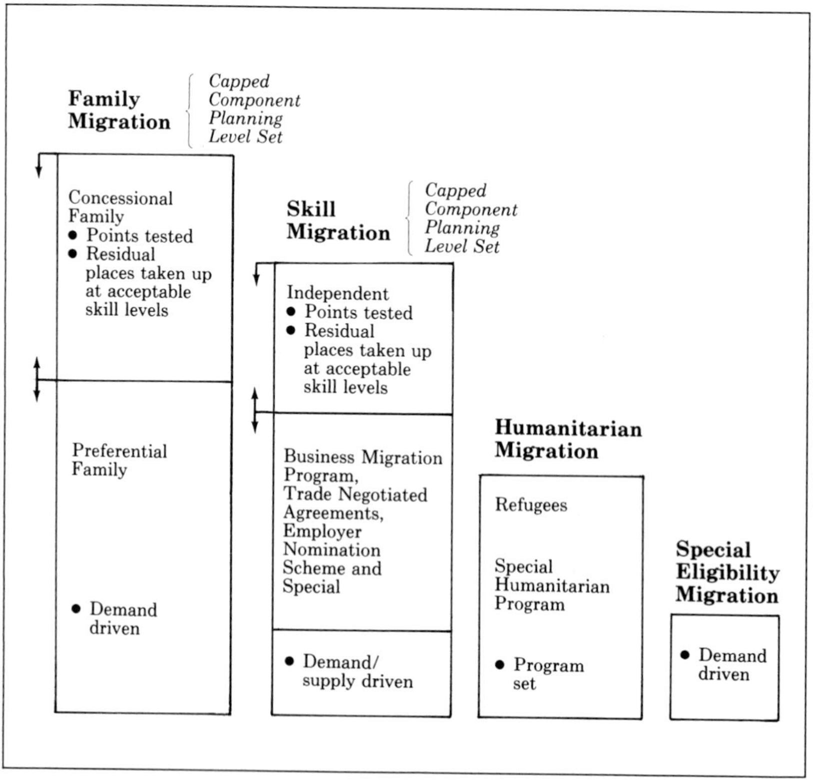

Source: Borowski & Shu 1992, p. 36.

fixed entities. They undergo modification in line with economic, political, social and other factors. For example, the target for 1992–93 was reduced to fewer than 100 000, for the first time since the early 1980s. This was achieved by a reduction in the skill categories.

It is useful to note here features of the contemporary program. As of June 1992, the aims of the immigration program can be described in the following terms (DILGEA 1992, p. 27).

The migration program regulates the flow of people into and out of Australia (although there is no visa requirement for New Zealand citizens). It includes both persons who apply overseas and are granted visas and persons who change status within Australia. The purpose is to balance the demands arising from:

❏ the need for skills to contribute to Australia's economy;

❏ the desire to recognise family migration; and

❏ the commitment to humanitarian goals.

This is reflected in the three main components: Family, Skill and Humanitarian migration. The Family and Skill Migration components are subject to capped planning levels. The points-tested Concessional Family and Independent categories take up residual places at acceptable skill levels once the demand-driven categories are filled.

Figure 2.1 shows most succinctly the structure of the immigration program.

Statistical profile of immigration numbers by gender

In order to see some of the effects of Australia's immigration policies in statistical terms, a brief overview is given of the numbers of women immigrants entering Australia in the period from 1947 to the present. Additional details such as immigration category, age group and source countries are provided for the last five-year period.

According to the 1986 Census, 1 582 902 women in Australia were born overseas. This represented 20.2 per cent of all Australian women, slightly lower than the proportion of men born overseas (21.4 per cent) (Madden & Young 1993b). Between 1965 and 1990, 2 729 390 persons arrived as settlers in Australia and 1 326 160 (48.6 per cent) of them were women. In the 1975–80 period, and since 1986, women have represented just over half the immigrant intake. For instance, in 1986–87 they were 50.9 per cent of a total 113 540 settlers. In 1987–88 women made up 50.1 per cent of the total 143 470 settler arrivals. Of the total settler arrivals (145 320) in 1988–89, women represented 50.2 per cent; and of 121 227 settler arrivals in 1989–90, 61 009 (50.3 per cent) were women (BIR 1991b).

For the 1989–90 period:

❑ According to Madden and Young (1993b), as shown in table 2.2, the largest source countries for women were the UK and Ireland (12 254), Viet Nam (5761), New Zealand (5420), Hong Kong (3996), the Philippines (3739) and Malaysia (3191). These were also the main source countries for men, although the order changes slightly with New Zealand and Viet Nam and also the Philippines and Malaysia reversed. The countries providing more than 1000 women, and where women represent more than 50.3 per cent of all settler arrivals from that country, were the Philippines (61.5 per cent), Viet Nam (51.6 per cent), Yugoslavia (51.4 per cent), Fiji (51.2 per cent), People's Republic of China (51.0 per cent) and Taiwan (50.3 per cent). Other countries with significantly higher intakes of women than men are Thailand (65.8 per cent), Romania (56.3 per cent) and Indonesia (55.3 per cent).

Table 2.2: Top ten source countries of birth for settler arrivals in 1989–90

Top ten 1989–90	Settler arrivals	Females (%)
UK and Ireland	25 591	47.9
New Zealand	11 178	48.5
Viet Nam	11 156	51.6
Hong Kong	8 054	49.6
Malaysia	6 417	49.7
China	6 124	50.7
Philippines	6 080	61.5
India	3 016	50.3
Fiji	2 632	51.2
South Africa	2 424	48.3
Subtotal	82 672	
Other	38 555	
Total	121 227	

Source: Madden & Young 1993b, p. 26.

❑ There was a greater proportion of women in the 50+ age group than men, that is, 9.7 per cent of all female settlers were in that age group (see table 2.3) compared with 9.1 per cent of all male settlers. The proportion of male settlers was greater than the proportion of female settlers in most other age groups; an interesting exception was the 20–29 group, where women of that age represented 25.2 per cent of all female settlers and men of that age represented 24.1 per cent of all male settlers (Madden & Young, 1993b).

Table 2.3: Age distribution of settler arrivals, 1989–90 (percentages)

	Settler arrivals	
Age (years)	*Male*	*Female*
0–9	19.9	19.2
10–19	15.3	15.3
20–29	24.1	25.2
30–39	22.4	22.1
40–49	9.2	8.5
50+	9.1	9.7
Total	100.0	100.0

Source: Madden & Young 1993b, p. 27.

❏ According to table 2.4, more women than men tend to enter under Family Migration categories, whereas more men than women tend to enter under all other categories. Further, the general tendency is for more men to enter under the Skill Migration category than under any other.

Table 2.4: Eligibility component and gender of settler arrivals, 1989–90

	Female		Male	
	Number	*%*	*Number*	*%*
Family	27 457	45.0	22 484	37.3
Skill	20 104	33.0	22 732	37.8
Humanitarian	5 417	8.9	6 531	10.8
Special Eligibility	8 031	13.1	8 471	14.1
Total	61 009	100.00	60 218	100.0

Source: Madden & Young 1993b, p. 30.

In sum, it can be seen that in very recent years there has been a trend towards a slight feminisation of the immigrant intake. In earlier periods, however, there was a more or less balanced intake, with only slightly fewer women. That marked overrepresentation of women to be found in some ethnic groups now, is seen as a concern by some. On the other hand, there is unlikely to be any definite gender shift in the total population unless feminisation continues and becomes significantly greater. There can be no general argument of discrimination against women immigrants over Australia's post-Second World War immigration history discerned from these general immigrant numbers. However, when the selection process is considered in detail, that generalisation may be able to be qualified.

A gendered immigration and selection policy

And this year 1969-70—our immigration program calls for the arrival of 175 000 settlers. To obtain these people, Australian migration officers serving in 25 countries will have handled around one million enquiries in 20 languages and interviewed more than 300 000 people . . . I am confident of the success of this vast operation. About half these new settlers will be workers, most of them married and accompanied by their wives and children. Many of these workers will be professionals, skilled tradesmen and other key workers. (Speech by Phillip Lynch, Minister for Immigration, 4 April 1970)

One of the most striking features of early immigration policy was the amount of discretion that could be applied by selection officers. Guidelines were brief, as though anticipating that applicants would be much alike and few would be rejected. As unforeseen situations arose over the years, a new guideline would be included and usually officers were advised to refer the case to Canberra for decision. Guidelines became increasingly sophisticated in their detail and the range of situations with which they were meant to deal. Correspondingly, Canberra delegated more decision-making power to the officers in the field. The end of the 'White Australia Policy' and the introduction of universally applied 'objective' criteria by means of numerical assessment reduced the degree of discretion of overseas officers although it was still considerable. Officers retained the power to be flexible, to waive some criteria or to take a strict or lenient approach. Therefore individual characteristics of officers could play their own part in determining the outcomes of Australia's immigration policy. A watershed in immigration policy was reached in December 1989 when the *Migration Act 1958* was substantially amended to incorporate selection criteria into legislation. This had the effect of further curtailing the discretionary powers of selection officers.

From our interviews with officers who had been posted overseas, several common views emerged. Officers acknowledged the degree of discretion they held. The more recently they were selecting overseas the less discretion they felt they had, with the exception of officers selecting under the Refugee and Special Humanitarian programs, who even today considered that their discretion was extensive. This was tempered, however, by a sense of duty, to discharge their functions at what they considered to be a departmental standard or in Australia's interest. These views are represented in the extracts from interview transcripts below, which are ordered chronologically according to the date of the experience to preserve the confidentiality of the sources. They indicate how the decline in amount of discretion was expressed by the officers.

We had quite a lot of discretion really, quite a lot, but we'd have to justify it. I guess I've always been a policy man, even though I might have been sympathetic to certain clients, if they didn't make it they didn't make it and I said so. You didn't have discretion to simply approve anybody. Just a wider border in which you could operate. (1968)

At that time there was a lot of discretion. I rapidly learnt, on writing reports that you don't expect the person above you to be objective. If I like your case I write all favourable things, if I'm going to say no to you, I build a very solid box and nail it down firmly, I don't say anything positive about the person. I had my own standards. I was an average person with average values and a bit of commonsense and was realistic about it. (1970)

The qualifications were assessed by a Technical Adviser who was seconded from the Department of Employment. So you really didn't have any discretion on the qualifications but you did have discretion on whether you felt they were going to settle. We made the decision and we also decided at the same time whether they should be given assisted passage. The particular way we had to decide it then would be described now as subjective. To a certain degree you set your own standard. (1975)

When NUMAS came in, the numerical one, I'd say we had less discretion and of course now you virtually have no discretion any more. If you thought they were worth going to Australia you could get them in, now you can't. Before NUMAS you still had that ability. I think a lot of it was commonsense. I think they thought that I was a reasonable Australian who wanted to keep my country looking reasonable. (1978)

All the migration arrangements were under policy which was just there as a guide. Although there was a points system as such, that was just a guide to the way in which applications had to be assessed. Most officers overseas, being professional migration officers would have followed those pretty closely. Not only was it in their interest to do so in having a professional operation at a post, but in terms of having consistent decision-making between posts. (1982)

We had a good deal more discretion than now but nonetheless I personally was inclined to treat even the policy circulars as something for which I could be made accountable in the long run. So I was only choosing people who, as far as I could see, clearly met the criteria and if they didn't clearly meet the criteria my colleague and I would talk to each other and if we couldn't agree amongst ourselves we might talk to the more senior person there. (1983)

The guidelines were very tight, we're not talking about a time when there was an enormous amount of discretion so the guidelines told you who you

21

were looking for and you just fitted each application into its box. I've said there wasn't much room for discretion. Well of course, there was. When you're deciding how educated someone is, or how skilled they are, there is, and you had a lot of use of judgment. We were very professional. I think the standard of decision-making generally was excellent and I think all of us had a very high sense of Australia's best interest. (1984)

Often you gave people the benefit of the doubt. There were some things you had to follow in the Migrant Entry Handbook. There was still interpretation in the old MEH though. We would still discuss among ourselves how something could be interpreted. (1986)

Before the regulations we had massive discretion. When you applied it was very rarely. When you're overseas you're there as an identity and you know that you're there to represent Australia's interests. (1988)

At the beginning we had quite a bit of discretion, before it became law, but when the law came our discretion was largely taken away. (1989)

But, on refugee selection, the situation remains somewhat different:

It wouldn't be too far to say discretion was total. There are no review mechanisms for these [refugee] decisions that I'm aware of. I felt that we were representatives of Australia and we were, in that sense, not only representatives but also representative. So I tried to take into account what I thought the average Australian would think. (1990)

Officers were asked what they were looking for in an immigrant and what they thought an 'ideal immigrant'. Most of them found it difficult to answer and attempted to list some of the characteristics which emerged from the selection criteria. Again, the comments of officers recorded below are listed according to the years those officers worked overseas, so chronological shifts in prevailing departmental interpretations can be observed. The shift in emphasis towards skills begins to be evident in these comments.

In those days we were looking for young educated migrants, educated enough to be useful in a manual, semi-skilled occupation. With young families, the emphasis was on the family unit. Young children who would assimilate and integrate into Australia, that was a very strong plus factor in the selection process. (1968)

Family units, for a preference, and workers, young people prepared to accept any work. We were looking for somebody thirty to thirty-five with a wife and a couple of kids because that was the stabilising factor. (1970)

Somebody with a reasonable employment record, no criminal background, no major illness and looked nice, clean and well presented. (1982)

The ideal migrant was the person in their twenties or thirties who had job skills and a bit of initiative. (1975)

I don't think there is any such thing as an ideal migrant. Somebody who is going to be economically viable, to get employment quickly, not have settlement problems and not get involved in any antisocial behaviour or any criminal activity or have any health problems. (1979)

I don't know that there was one. (1982)

I think the ideal would have been a young couple, loaded with money, with high levels of skills who were going to come into Australia needing everything, having nothing thereby creating all the growth that Australia ever needed. (1984)

Young, educated, who spoke good English, I would say. People who could go straight into the work force without any concerns at all. (1986)

Young skilled person or family who spoke English well who was looking to give something to Australia. (1988)

At the beginning it was really somebody who was going to settle in Australia, was well educated and had a good work history and if they had a family that was even better still. But in the end it seemed to be people who had an occupation that was in demand and was young. (1990)

For the remainder of this section, answers are sought to the questions: In the immigration context, have women been assessed as having 'desirable' traits? How have they met the selection criteria? What have been the factors constraining and enabling their selection as immigrants? Our concern here is to ask, in the interests of gender equity, how immigrant women fared in relation to immigrant men in the selection processes.

We identify two periods since the Second World War, during which views of the 'ideal male and female immigrant' underpinning immigration policies and procedures seem to have differed. Immediately after the war, Australia's immigration intake was built around able-bodied, male, manual workers from Europe. Immigration Department officers overseas recruited such men. Immigrant women in this period were viewed in relation to the masculine ideal immigrant. They were dependants, their status as immigrants relying on their marital and familial characteristics rather than 'skills' or physical strength, though women's age was an important eligibility criterion because it affected their capacity to bear children. By the 1980s, certain definitions of skill were emerging to define the ideal immigrant, replacing the emphasis on physical stature of the previous period. But, as they had been in their relationship to earlier views of the desirable, male, physical characteristics of immigrants, so again with the skill-based definitions of the ideal immigrant, women were marginalised. The desired occupational characteristics associated with being 'skilled' were those most commonly held by men, as those of physical stature had been before them.

Accordingly, 'immigrant' has been a gendered category in Australian immigration policy since the Second World War (see Kunek 1989). The visions of masculinity and femininity suffusing immigrant selection in these two sets of post-war decades are evident in the following material presented.

Women and the masculine ideal immigrant

A 1956 poster of an Italian cane cutter with the caption 'There's a man's job waiting for you' evokes the focus on male bodies in Australian immigrant selection in the immediate post-Second World War period. Australia actively recruited young, able-bodied *men* from overseas to work in agriculture, mining and on major construction projects. Displaced persons from Central Europe, tradesmen from Britain and rural workers from Southern Europe immigrated under the major programs of the day to fill a labour shortage in Australia. An officer posted to Britain in 1948 describes Australia's masculine 'needs':

> We were basically looking for anybody who could make a contribution, particularly physically, towards the development of industries. People who didn't qualify were virtually the lame, the old and the blind. (Martin 1989, p. 15)

'Migrant' became synonymous with 'worker', but with a male worker in a manual job. Two consequences emerged—on the one hand, the masculinisation of the Australian immigrant population and on the other, the marginalisation of women in the immigration program. A 1969 Immigration Department report explains:

> There was a preponderance of males in the early years of Australia's post-war migration programme due to the influx of refugees, mainly single males; to large-scale unassisted migration from Southern Europe which initially was largely male; and to early tendencies to recruit single men to build up the work force with minimum demands on housing and other services. (Department of Immigration File 69/70582)

In these early days, handbooks or manuals were compiled to advise Australian immigration officers overseas, or Foreign Affairs representatives fulfilling immigration tasks, on assessment of applicants. Their subject headings itemised characteristics of immigrant workers such as age, physical bearing and occupation. As the perceived attributes of women were included, the headings relating to them were added, focusing entirely on their marital, moral and familial status, for example: 'Married women', 'Single women', 'Divorcees with children', 'Legally separated women', 'Unaccompanied women'. These headings speak for themselves—immigrant women were characterised by their marital status and relationship to a male immigrant.

Before 1979, as we have noted, immigration officers were acting on a general and personal knowledge of what was required by Australia. A broad pre-departure training program infused them with a view of Australia's 'needs', and regular circulars and 'labour requisition' notices gave them the specifics of the occupations of immigrants required to fill gaps in the Australian labour force. One officer interviewed said:

We went all over Australia and we talked to various organisations that employed migrants so we had an idea of what was wanted in Australia at the time. (1968)

Reading through the manuals of 1959 to 1972, one gets a very definite idea of what Australian policy-makers expected an immigrant to be. *Young, white, able bodied* and *male* emerge as the attributes of the intended model immigrant. Many of the subsections of the manuals discuss personal characteristics to give guidance on whether an applicant fitted the mould. Such matters as age, nationality, family status, marital status, height, cleanliness, health and character are all dealt with. These change little over these years, with a few exceptions. The 1964 handbook refers to 'sound migration gain' and 'good migration gain', although these terms are given no concrete definition. In context, they appear to refer to ideal families which consist of one breadwinner, one wife and a couple of children:

All applicants and their families should be above average for the area in which they are living having regard to appearance, manner and dress. Families which represent a particularly good migration gain can be given special consideration even though the breadwinner may not normally be acceptable on occupational grounds.

Age was an important policy criterion in 1959; the age requirement was 18 to 45 for single men and 18 to 35 for single women. Married couples without children also had to be under 45 and those with minor children were accepted up to the age of 50. Engaged women coming to Australia to marry were not bound by an upper age limit, while men immigrating to marry their Australian fiancées had to be between 18 and 45 years. Other sponsored relatives, such as parents, had no age limit. In 1972, while the recommended upper age limit for single women remained 35, officers were urged when assessing single women over 35 years 'to be mindful of the policy of encouraging women of marriageable age to migrate'. An officer recollects:

Single person without a sponsor—there might have been a 35 age limit, women are beyond child-bearing years usually at 35, back in those old-fashioned days. (1970)

It was not until 1976 that the upper age limit for single women was brought into line with that of single men and raised to 45 years. The introduction of a numerical scoring system at the end of the 1970s reinforced this upper age by not allotting points to any person over 45 years. Now in legislation, this practice remains the same.

The size and physical attributes criterion is an indicator of the emphasis on labourers and manual workers in the early post-Second World War period and may also be an indication that notions of population-building were tied up with the belief that Australia needed more men in order to defend against military invasion. Up until the mid-1970s, all applicants were to be screened for shortness in case their height might prevent them from working or cause them to be scorned by the Australian public. When interviewing for suitability the manuals recommended that:

> For persons within the worker age group, the assessment should take into account—
>
> (b) general physique in relation to occupation. An applicant should not be of such diminutive size and/or poor physique as to be at a distinct disadvantage in competing in a new environment for employment in his normal occupation. (1971)

Here it appears the emphasis was on employability; however, in 1964 officers were advised that the height limit could be disregarded if the immigrant 'possesses a skill unaffected by a lack of height' or on compassionate grounds as long as:

> (b) the person concerned must be otherwise of robust build and not such diminutive size as to provoke adverse comment in a normal Australian community; and
>
> (c) where a family unit is involved the lack of height must be confined to one or two members depending on the number of persons in the family and it must be clear that the degree of shortness is not a familial trait.

An immigration officer:

> You had to be five foot tall ... the reason for that was five foot was the entrance to the Australian army ... Even if they were very short if they looked as if they were used to outdoor work, we used to say to people are you prepared to accept any work? And they would say yes.

Literacy in one's own language has always been a requirement for the immigration of those presumed to be entering the Australian work force. In the immediate post-Second World War period, it was another characteristic by which men were distinguished from women in the immigration selection process. It was not anticipated that women would enter the work force, so the selection manuals excluded them, along with their children, from the requirement to undertake a literacy test. This was spelt out in the 1976 manual:

> With the exception of sponsored spouses, dependent children and parents who would not be entering the workforce, all persons 16 years of age and over are required to be literate.

The policy guidelines were not necessarily applied to the letter and immigration officers who had a large degree of discretion under the guidelines of the time might apply their own standard of literacy:

> If any member of the family wasn't literate in their own language then in those days they were simply rejected, and the spouse. (1968)

Another officer:

> You could refuse a person if they were illiterate. The Principal Applicant had to do it, and the spouse, you tested both. Rejection could only be based on the Principal Applicant. If the wife was illiterate it should be recorded but that in itself was not enough to debar it. A fiancée didn't get tested, they were just breeding material. (1970)

And another:

Literacy, I don't think, was a requirement for spouses. We had spouses coming in and they couldn't read and they couldn't write. (1982)

In spite of literacy standards continuing to exempt most women, in a letter to the Assistant Secretary of Programme Control and Development dated 19 March 1975, the chief migration officer, Beirut, stated:

I am of course aware of the particular problem of illiterate wives plus children coming from Lebanon to join their husbands in Australia . . . Many girls in these families are obliged to work in the house or on the land as soon as they are able and are not sent to school . . . the situation often arises where the wife is illiterate (she is only supposed to be a good housewife) and the question of illiteracy is not important in *their* eyes. This situation is slowly changing but there is a long way to go . . . all applicants including husbands and wives are given a simple literacy test but up to the present it has not been the practice to reject an applicant solely on the basis of a wife's illiteracy . . . Illiteracy is a disqualifying factor for breadwinners, single males and females. (Department of Immigration File 74/77682; our emphasis)

On the issue of illiteracy among some sponsored women immigrants, a Department memo dated 7 February 1975 indicated a re-examination of the view that women immigrants could be illiterate:

In the decade following the Second World War when we were very concerned to maximise our 'settler' intake, our search for available migrants took us into a number of countries, where, at the time there was considerable illiteracy . . . It was a time when it was reasonable to assume that only a very small proportion of the female migrant intake would enter the Australian workforce, that migrant wives would tend to be engaged almost exclusively on 'home duties' and that sponsored fiancées would almost automatically soon become such wives . . . Today we have a very different situation. We are more concerned to contain rather than expand our 'settler' entry, females constitute a large and important sector of the Australian workforce, and the global fight against illiteracy has made gigantic strides over the past quarter of a century.

By the 1989 Migrant Entry Handbook, literacy was still a requirement for all but applicants under the Preferential Family category. However, it appears that, with the introduction of a points scoring system of assessment, the assessment of literacy was submerged in the educational attainment and English competency components of the Principal Applicant's assessment. The purpose of the points system was to assess the ability of the Principal Applicant to enter and contribute to the labour force and so attributes of the spouse or children were not taken into account. The purpose, as stated in the Migrant Entry Handbook, was to assess 'the applicant's employability and settlement prospects'. The current points system, for Independent and Concessional Family categories, while using different criteria for assessment, still focuses on the economic and labour force contribution of the Principal Applicant as the litmus test for successful immigration. Literacy requirements have disappeared.

Women and the family unit

We have broadly characterised the twenty-five years after the Second World War as a period of immigrant selection when women were not expected to work in paid employment, and when 'skills' (including literacy and physical strength) were assessed only for men. All through this period, however, were sprinkled concerns with 'economic viability' and the skills that could ensure this, that occasionally included women and the sorts of labour market slots they could fill. The occasional statements about the work force contributions of immigrant women were largely offset by women's and children's perceived drain on families' economic viability.

A 1976 handbook describes the 'basic requirements' of a person seeking to immigrate. This statement outlines the principle behind the criteria of previous years. Other than intending to settle permanently and being of good health and character, an immigrant must:

> be assessed as being economically viable in Australia . . . The term 'economic viability' is defined as being related to an applicant's ability to earn a living in Australia in his chosen field and his ability to maintain himself and, where applicable, his family to a suitable standard.

In the way they were included in early concepts of the family unit used in immigration selection, women were clearly envisaged as dependants with little capacity to make an economic contribution to support their relatives. The 'family unit' is an important concept in immigration policy. It refers to all those who, on the basis of one applicant's successful selection, are also eligible for immigration. While only the Principal Applicant is required to satisfy primary criteria, all members of the 'family unit' are required to satisfy general criteria such as health and character. Should one member of the 'family unit' fail to meet the general criteria, the whole unit is refused.

In 1959 'family unit' referred to a 'husband', 'wife', 'unmarried minor sons' and 'unmarried minor daughters'. An unmarried man or woman aged over 18 was considered not to have a family. For the purposes of being sponsored by an Australian resident, in 1959 parents were not considered dependent if they had an adult son living in the same country. This presumed that adult sons could support their parents, though not adult daughters. By 1964 the concept of 'dependent relative' had been added to the manual. This was defined explicitly as 'wives and minor children', already part of the family unit, and also included parents where the father was over 65 and had no adult son in his country of residence and where the mother was widowed or divorced and had no adult son in her country of residence.

The year 1964 also saw the inclusion of a statement that 'single dependent daughters' need not be minors. Alongside the economics of who in a family unit was dependent and who supported them, were strong moral views about people (women exclusively) who were not part of these 'normal' families. For instance, in the 1960s there were requirements for maintenance guarantees to be made by male relatives, for separate accommodation for men and women, for additional checks on married women who wanted to travel without their husbands, either for a visit or immigration. Financial assistance to unpartnered women with children was to be refused. This suggests that the policy-makers of the day worked on the presumption that women had strong moral and immoral influences on a society.

Some specific indicators: in a letter to the Department Secretary in 1956, the Chief of Mission of the Intergovernmental Committee for European Migration, Canberra, commented:

> I still think that the safest immigration is the one caused by nominations of migrants already in Australia. After all, a nomination engages the legal responsibility of the nominator and this goes a long way towards avoiding possible dangers of mis-use of assistance to bring in females who could be used as prostitutes. (Department of Immigration File 65/46611)

Under the heading 'Legally separated women' the 1964 manual advised officers to:

> reject nominations for legally separated women lodged by male non-relatives in Australia where it is considered that a de facto union would result, except . . . approve such nominations where a de facto union existed before the sponsor came here and there are children of the union.

The then Minister, Mr A. R. Downer, commented on this policy on 13 February 1960:

> An immigration policy which smiles on illicit unions would not be in the interests of the Good Life of the Australian community. Those who wish to live in such a way, should not expect an easy entry into this country. (Department of Immigration File 72/77443)

Although the Advisory Committee had made the point when considering a policy on 'legally separated women' in 1957 that 'the Department is not obliged or entitled to act as a custodian of morals', a strong moral stance was taken by the Minister and by the Department, which continued until the seventies when de facto marriages were considered on compassionate grounds.

In 1972 'family unit' was defined as the spouse and unmarried children under 21 years and in 1976 the definition was reworded as the 'visa applicant and his dependants'. In 1982 'family unit' had resumed the 'husband, wife and minor unmarried children' definition which, according to the Principles of Immigration Policy outlined in the 1982 Migrant Entry Handbook, is the 'Australian norm'.

Later in the 1980s, a reworking of the inclusion of aged parents in the family unit eligible for immigration is evident. The 'Balance of

Family Test' was introduced in 1989 to limit the number of aged parents being sponsored to Australia by their immigrant children. The test is that a parent over the retirement age should have at least an equal number of children, if not more, in Australia compared with overseas to be eligible to immigrate. No longer does this single out daughters as economically incapable. The test still applies, as does the concept of 'aged dependent relative' being a relative, over the retirement age, who is substantially supported by the applicant or sponsor. The legal definition of a 'dependent child', introduced in December 1989 and still current, is one who is not engaged to be married or a spouse and is under 18; or is 18 or over and dependent; or is incapacitated for work. An aged dependent relative must be single, over the retirement age and dependent. In both contexts 'dependent' is defined as substantially requiring the financial, physical or psychological support of the sponsor or Principal Applicant but no longer is specified in terms of sex.

Women as breadwinners or Principal Applicants

Policy discussions of immigrants' physical or skill capacities that have made them able to contribute to Australian industrial growth in the post-Second World War period, have been accompanied also by discussions of who in immigrant family units would be principal earner, and financial supporter of that family unit. In the early period, 'breadwinners' were the identified individuals and breadwinners were, by policy definition, male. Later, the term Principal Applicant emerged, which is gender-neutral in its definition, although, in practice, applicants for migration selection may not have interpreted it so.

While the earlier manuals used the term 'applicant', 'breadwinner' was also a common reference to applicants with dependent family members. Other than the use of the pronoun 'he' to refer to 'applicants', a clue to the gender of the 'breadwinner' lies in the 1964 manual dealing with 'Dependants unaccompanied by breadwinner' in which it is stated:

> a member of the family unit of an applicant or nominee should not be permitted to proceed to Australia ahead of the breadwinner but a breadwinner may be permitted to precede his dependants. The consent of a wife to the issue of a visa to her husband is not required in such cases.

An immigration officer stationed in Europe in the late 1960s discussed the size of the program in these terms:

> we managed to get, first up, 200 breadwinners plus family, so about 1000 migrants that we had to select. (1968)

'Head of family unit' was interchangeable with 'breadwinner', while 'married woman' was interchangeable with 'dependant' in discussions of the eligibility for entry of wives and minor dependent children.

The 1972 manual makes it clear that 'breadwinner' and wife are mutually exclusive terms:

a married woman should not be granted a visa to enable her to travel to Australia ahead of her husband although a husband or breadwinner may precede his dependants.

Although the pronoun 'he' was used universally until the late 1980s, other gender-specific language was removed from the handbooks about 1976. 'Spouse' was employed to replace 'wife' or 'husband', and 'person' replaced man or woman. While the language began to change during the late 1970s, the policy had not, hence:

Where an Australian resident or citizen sponsors his spouse for migration . . . Officers must be satisfied that the applicant and spouse will be able to support themselves and their children. This will be fulfilled if the sponsor:

- is . . . in full-time employment or in receipt of equivalent income from private sources, or

- is in receipt of an age or invalid pension.

In some cases, the Australian processing office will ask the overseas post to assess the sponsored spouse's ability to provide support, but in most cases it is the sponsoring spouse's ability to provide support that will be assessed.

This is a 1982 interpretation of the previous policy of 'breadwinners' sponsoring their wives and children on the condition that they can support them. 'In some cases' presumably refers to the hitherto infrequent occurrence of women sponsoring their male spouses.

The term 'Principal Applicant' came into use in the mid-1980s and refers to an individual applicant for immigration or one member of the family unit. It is basically an administrative device, still in use, by which an immigration application can be identified. In general, the Principal Applicant is the person whose name first appears in the application form. That person should also be the applicant whose circumstances best satisfy the selection criteria; however, this is not always the case. As the application form is completed by the applicant, she or he decides who to put in the first part of the form. That name is usually used for filing purposes, while it is common practice by immigration assessing officers, under most categories, to check the eligibility of all members included in the application. While women were clearly excluded from the earlier 'breadwinner' category, they are quite admissible as 'Principal Applicants' from an Australian policy point of view. But as officers pointed out:

In sponsorship cases, as far as we were concerned the Principal Applicant was the one who had the relative in Australia but that wasn't always the case as far as the applicants were concerned. They may well have put down the male on the application form as the Principal Applicant even though it was his wife who had relatives. (1983)

> If it was a family usually the male would just automatically put himself down as the Principal Applicant on the form but we looked at both parties and just selected who had the best chance. (1986)
>
> I would interview the Principal Applicant who is normally the man of the family but not always. The Principal Applicant really is a bit of a nonsense term because all it means is the person who fills in the application form. (1988)

By 1989 the concepts of family unit, Principal Applicant and dependence had been resolved thus:

> Because members of a principal applicant's family unit derive their eligibility from the principal applicant and may also be dependent upon the principal applicant, they are not to enter Australia in advance of the principal applicant.

The circumstances of women as Principal Applicants have, however, to be examined as they appear in the different immigration policy entry categories (see figure 2.1).

Principal Applicants are the immigrants who meet Australia's eligibility requirements. Their family units make up the immigrants who enter as their dependants. Therefore, successful female Principal Applicants have established an independent entitlement to immigrate. But when the categories are broken down, it can be seen that the majority of female Principal Applicants enter because of their family relationships, as aged mothers, last remaining relatives, carers, wives, daughters and fiancées and that they have far less success than their male counterparts in economically assessed categories. This is not to say that in the 1980s and 1990s women have less predilection to immigrate than men.

> Often the application form would be filled in by the wife. Maybe it was because the wife wasn't working and the husband was, or maybe it was because the wife could write better. That was probably the main reason why that was done. Or maybe it was because our program was seen as a bit of a lottery ticket and if you put in your free lottery ticket and you won well that was well and good. I think it was, 'this is all very hard, we can't earn any money, life's pretty hard, I'm going to put in an application to go to Australia or Canada', usually both. (1988)

To illustrate, settler arrivals in 1989–90 (see table 2.5) included 28 253 Principal Applicants in the Family Migration component (comprising the Concessional and Preferential Family categories). Just over half, 14 521, were women. Of 15 763 Principal Applicants in the Skill Migration component, only 3266 (20.7 per cent) were women. Of all settler arrivals, that is Principal Applicants and their family units, females make up just over half: 47 722 compared with 45 215 males. The breakdown by eligibility category indicates how more women enter under the Family component than men and more men than women enter under the Skilled component.

One reservation when interpreting the statistics on Principal Applicants is that more married women may have met the eligibility

Table 2.5: Settler arrivals by sex and visa category by
Principal/accompanying for financial year 1989-90

	Principal	Accompanying	Total
1989-90 male			
Family Migration			
Preferential	8 726	3 335	12 061
Concessional	4 994	5 429	10 423
Skill Migration	12 497	10 234	22 731
1989-90 female			
Family Migration			
Preferential	12 382	5 591	17 973
Concessional	2 139	7 308	9 447
Skill Migration	3 266	16 838	20 104
1989-90 total			
Family Migration	28 241	21 663	49 904
Skill Migration	15 763	27 072	42 835
Grand total	44 004	48 735	92 739

Source: Data from BIPR Statistics Section.

criteria than are shown, but they or their husbands have listed the male partner as the Principal Applicant. For example:

> Male Lebanese were significantly more likely to feel that, as a male, they had an advantage because the male is seen as the traditional head of the family and is the breadwinner. (Madden & Young 1993b, pp. 102-3).

Likewise, in the Concessional Family category, which requires the sponsorship of a relative in Australia, the wife may be listed as Principal Applicant because she has the Australian relative, but it is her husband's occupational qualifications which make up the greater part of the points allocation. Therefore, although a general picture emerges, to obtain the precise detail of how women fare under our immigration selection criteria, it would be necessary to survey the applications on file with a view to discovering whether these phenomena are common.

> One Malaysian man married to an equally skilled Malaysian wife said *he* was told by the immigration authorities that he would be the Principal Applicant. A British immigrant, whose husband was the Principal Applicant said 'The official kept asking me questions but then looked at my husband while I answered.' (Madden & Young 1993b, p. 102)

Two female officers made their own attempts at listing wives as Principal Applicants:

With me at that post the person who was most likely to be eligible became the Principal Applicant but often that was a male. (1983)

Regardless of the skills of the female the Principal Applicant was almost always the male. If there was a stenographer and a fitter and the man was the fitter it would be almost inevitable that he'd be made the Principal Applicant, even if people like I tried to stop that. You might often put on the top of the form the Principal Applicant's name and give the woman's name and details and find that it had come back to you changed by a locally engaged staff member. (1984)

Independent women, married or single, wanting to immigrate may well have been rare in many of the source countries of earlier days. This was certainly the impression gained by immigration officers overseas in the late 1960s:

Women have a role there in these countries that aren't terribly developed. The emphasis is on traditionally the man being the breadwinner. He's the one who goes out hunting and keeps the family together and the wife creates a home. And single women lived with the family until they were married. They went from family to husband . . . There were very few independent women of working age. We would probably get some in Madrid or Barcelona, in the more sophisticated urban areas. But they'd be regarded more as an oddity. (1968)

And:

In Italy I don't know what skill a single woman would have acquired because there weren't enough jobs for men.

I never met a male child raiser with two children under ten and his wife was a professional, I just never met one, I don't think any existed. (1969)

However, other factors may also have been at work during that period of greater subjective and discretionary assessment, factors which may have discriminated against female 'breadwinners' or Principal Applicants. An officer posted to London suggests:

From memory the only women who were getting through in their own right were people with secretarial qualifications and nursing and teaching qualifications. Sometimes the Principal Applicant could be the wife. The husband wouldn't get in on his job skill so they would look up the job demand and see that secretaries were in demand so you'd get the wife applying on the basis of her secretarial skills. She may not have worked as a secretary since she got married so she'd been out of the work force sometimes for fifteen years so you mightn't approve it on that basis because she didn't have any employment history to base her claims on. But if she had been working, it might only be a part-time job, then you could go ahead on that qualification. But then you had to look at the husband who wasn't in those days, in the 1970s, prepared to have his wife support him and if he was going to be disgruntled because he couldn't get a job that was something you did take into account. So I suppose it was tougher for women to get through than it would have been with the man with the skills. And they also weren't going to be able to keep a family on a secretarial wage so that's what you looked at too. (1984)

Economic viability and single or married women

In assessing 'economic viability', an officer was asked to take into account the occupation of the applicant and likelihood of finding employment, whether the applicant had funds for transfer, any maintenance guarantee lodged by relatives in Australia and the size of the applicant's family. These aspects were areas for assessment before the term 'economic viability' entered the manuals. The 1976 manual described an immigrant or immigrant family as a 'worthwhile gain' if they were 'economically viable' and adaptable to the Australian community.

Policies could be modified by letter to overseas posts in order to alter the composition of the immigrant intake according to Australia's short-term economic needs. Certain categories of applicant could expediently be included or excluded, depending on the level of need, and thus become a 'good migration gain'. In a memo to the Assistant Secretary, Operations Branch, in March 1964, regarding Yugoslav refugees, it was stated:

> Recently the Secretary, Department of Labour and National Service stated that a shortage of unskilled workers was developing in Australia, a statement since endorsed by the Rt Hon. Harold Holt. Mr Bland also mentioned that the unskilled vacancies occurring were not generally of a type attractive to British migrants. Mr Bland has also advocated that we should give priority in recruitment to single male workers . . . Having regard to the factors involved it is felt we could now lift the restriction on under 21 refugees . . . (Department of Immigration File 63/46044).

Again, in the section of the 1970 handbook dealing with 'European aliens' the emphasis for selection is on the occupation of the applicant, with exceptions:

> Unskilled workers should only be accepted if it is considered that they (and their families) represent a distinct migration gain and that they will become self-supporting in the Australian community within a reasonable period.

The 1971 handbook for British consulates undertaking Australian immigration work sheds some light on this concept when it advises that applicants are:

> considered to represent a positive migration gain to Australia by reason of their trade, professional or like qualifications, personal attributes, family considerations, or other factors that would influence their contribution as migrants to Australia's economic and general development . . .

Large families, being two parents with more than four children, were not considered economically viable. Where they were accepted into the program, they were offered less assistance than a smaller family and, as this extract from a 1972 manual shows, they were expected to provide their own fares and accommodation and have more than one 'worker':

> Families with more than four children should not be accepted for assisted passages . . . unless [they can arrange private accommodation or] . . .

(c) there is in a family with five children one worker among the children and with six children there are two workers (preferably but not necessarily male—normally 16 years of age and over . . .) among the children. The wife's earning potential is not to be taken into account when determining the number of workers in a family.

One immigration officer interpreted this policy:

Economically we had to look at the number of children. Up to four we didn't query it, after that we'd see what sort of economic future they'd have in Australia . . . because many Anglo-Indians were Christians, basically Catholic, you know they had large families, ten, twelve children was not uncommon. Economically they were not really viable. (1972)

It is evident from the criteria laid out in the manuals over this period that women were not regarded as 'workers', were dealt with in terms of their relationship to male immigrants, that is as wives, sisters or daughters, and were considered dependent on male immigrants. That is not to say that the policy-makers of the day were not aware that wives did undertake paid work:

if a large family appears acceptable, the following information [should be] obtained—

(e) whether the wife intends to work in Australia and if so, in what capacity, and what experience she has had . . . (1972)

It can only be assumed that little worth was attributed then to the economic value of a wife's paid work or it was believed that childminding responsibilities were likely to preclude her from entering the paid work force.

After the introduction of points assessment, economic viability became one factor against which points were allocated as part of the overall 'economic/employment assessment'. A woman without a man to provide for her and with children to support was definitely not 'economically viable' according to this advice in a 1972 manual:

Even though a family with only one parent may appear to be a desirable migration gain, the difficulties likely to be encountered in settlement, the earning capacity of the breadwinner, and the care proposed for the children during working hours should be taken into consideration.

An immigration officer:

Say a widow with three kids, virtually economically it wasn't on, we didn't have child care facilities. (1970)

Another immigration officer recalling the case of a single woman with two children:

We approved the case, she was a secretary . . . she spoke impeccable English . . . there was no problem there, once her qualifications were recognised. I mean, mostly they were qualified and were employable and were young enough, then sure, that [being a single mother] was no restriction. (1972)

Although economic viability was an important criterion in choosing immigrants for Australia, it was of course not the only one. Sometimes other criteria could be used to enhance women's selection, even if economic criteria did not. Officers were conscious of the population-building and social-construction aspects of the immigration program. An officer:

> We were getting people with families, even if the breadwinners and their spouses weren't ideal in terms of what we were looking for, if they had three or four healthy children of school age, that made that family unit a worthwhile unit. (1968)

Therefore, children were a desirable immigration gain and single women, preferably without children, were also sometimes selected 'in the national interest'. This is pointed to by the decision, in 1969, to relax the policy on single women (that is divorced, widowed or unmarried, with children) so that they could be accepted under the Assisted Passage scheme, if nominated by a relative in Australia. In a memo to the Assistant Secretary, Operations Branch, one adviser stated:

> For some time now we have accepted the fact that women without breadwinners but with dependent children are not automatically ineligible for consideration for assisted passages. (1968)

The decision to relax the policy on 'Divorcees, widows, widowers and unmarried mothers with dependent children' was made by the Minister on 26 April 1968 in response to a Minute in which the Secretary advised that:

> There is one major reason why . . . [these categories] have been regarded as generally ineligible for assisted passages as Commonwealth nominees. All Commonwealth nominees are entitled on arrival to initial accommodation in hostels. Clearly, these categories would create special problems if admitted to hostels.
>
> In relation to unsponsored unassisted migration, it was considered that with no sponsors to accommodate and otherwise help them these people would normally be faced with serious accommodation and employment problems upon arrival in Australia. (Department of Immigration File 74/77192)

The Secretary went on to advise that as some cases could arise where applicants could be self-supporting and find their own accommodation, policy should be more lenient. As one Chief Migration Officer commented in a note of 6 May 1969:

> As I see it this is part of the move to bring more women of marriageable age to Australia . . . (Department of Immigration File 74/77192)

Since 1982, when 'family incomes' as well as 'size and composition of the family group' and 'ages and degree of dependence of the children', were still parts of the 'economic viability' assessment, all such aspects have been phased out of points assessment schemes. In the 1990s, only age, language ability and occupation of the Principal Applicant (in the independent and concessional categories) are taken into consideration.

Immigration Department interest in the 1960s in bringing marriageable single women to Australia did include the question of paid employment opportunities for immigrant women. This was a time of one of the rare mentions in policy thinking of immigrant women as potential paid work force members and contributors. It was recognised that a broader range of employment opportunities and better accommodation might make immigration to Australia more attractive to single women, this recognition coming after a period in which the program had not, numerically, been very successful. A Committee recommended that:

> Single girls should be selected overseas on the same basis as single men, i.e., that of their being able to secure employment on arrival in Australia and, wherever practicable, should be given vocational training and orientation courses prior to embarkation ... Employer and employee organisations, as well as training bodies, should assist in widening job opportunities for women. (Department of Immigration File 69/72633)

On the employment recommendation the following limited action was taken:

> We wrote to the Department of Labour and National Service asking for comments on the recommendation, especially on whether employer and employee groups, as well as training bodies, could help widen female job opportunities. That Department advised that comprehensive efforts are being made in this field, and that there are generally plenty of jobs available for women, including migrant women ... No further action is envisaged at present. (Department of Immigration File 69/72663)

An earlier program to introduce greater numbers of single women included women in the worker requisition allocations from Spain, Italy and Greece, as pointed out in this Departmental report of 1965:

> In order to redress the balance a number of policy measures have been taken over the years, e.g. ...
>
> (b) annual programmes to accept young women as domestics or hospital/ institutional employees from Spain, Italy and Greece under Assisted Passage procedures.

However, the 'requisition for Italian migrant workers' for the period February to December 1964 requisitioned a total of 2250 workers in various occupational categories:

> 250 are in Group B (Metal and Electrical Trades ...), 500 in Group C (Other Skilled and Semi-Skilled) and 1,500 in Group D (Unskilled). As regards Group D ... this includes 500 to be specially selected for the Broken Hill Proprietary for work primarily at Port Kembla though some would also be required at Whyalla and Newcastle. Of the remaining 1,000, at least 500 should be selected as suitable for sugar cane harvesting ...
>
> Aside from Group D where the emphasis should be on single men, we should provide generally for single men, married couples, and those with small families. (Department of Immigration File 63/46044)

The requisition forms were separated into occupational groups with total numbers for each group, and in a subsequent form were separated again into specific occupations. The list shows subgroups, among others under Group C, 'Skilled and semi-skilled clothing and textile' with the note, 'Male or female workers may be recruited in these categories' as well as 'Hospital workers (female only)' and 'Clerical and sales' which was separated into three occupations: 'Male clerical or sales worker under 35 years of age'; 'Female clerical or sales worker under 35 years of age' and 'Female stenographer and/or typist office machinist under 35 years of age'. The 'Hospital workers' were separated into two occupations, Wardsmaid and Nurse. Group E consisted of one occupation—'Domestics (single females only)'. Of the 2250 workers requisitioned from Italy for that period the total number of women accepted (from those categories for which they could be accepted) was nil.

Working women from the United Kingdom fared a little better in 1963, more for being women than for working, as this letter from the Department to the Acting Secretary, Department of Labour and National Service, dated 13 September 1963, attests:

> Thank you for your letter ... concerning the Requisition provision for female clerical and sales workers from the United Kingdom.
>
> I note that you would be disposed to agree to the movement of up to 200 such workers for arrival ... if this Department felt an increase above the 125 figure ... was necessary on *social and allied grounds* and provided that the female workers concerned are encouraged to go to Sydney or Melbourne where the employment situation is more favourable. (Department of Immigration File 63/46044, our emphasis)

From Greece, for the same July to December 1963 period, was a requisition for '5 hospital workers', '210 unskilled male workers' and '525 domestics' with the note, 'The provision for hospital workers has been made to cover the eventuality that single females qualified for this work become available'.

The total number of workers requisitioned world wide for the July to December 1963 program was 10 005, of which there were a possible 180 clothing and textile workers, 105 wardsmaids, 100 nurses, 5 possible bookbinders, 200 clerical or sales workers, 100 stenographers, typists or office machinists under 35 years of age and 1000 domestics. That is, a sum of 1690 possible occupational positions for women were included in the 1963 requisition, or just under 17 per cent of the total. It is interesting to note that these worker requisitions were made explicitly on the basis of birthplace as well as gender. Once the Department of Employment had designated labour shortages, the Immigration Department selected countries as recruiting sites for specific shortages, and determined the (limited) categories in which women could be sought as workers. These practices are examples of the stereotypes about immigrants that actually engineered, in a small way, their labour market segmentation once in Australia (see chapter 4).

While the high employment period of the mid-1960s brought about an increased demand for female labour, according to the Department

39

of Labour's figures, the demand remained in those areas designated as female occupations. Correspondingly, there was an increase in female unemployment rates, suggesting some resistance by women against entering those limited and poorly remunerated occupations. In 1966 it was reported that:

> The demand for female labour has remained strong over the past two years. The Statistician's figures . . . show that in the twelve months ending July 1966, female employment increased by 43 700 (4.1%), which although smaller than the increase in the twelve months ended July 1965 (57 900 or 5.8%), was nevertheless a faster rate of growth than for males . . . The demand for female workers in the clothing and textile industries remains strong . . . The demand for female workers suitable for hotel, guesthouse, and private domestic occupations continues to be strong particularly in Victoria and New South Wales. (Department of Immigration File 67/70369)

A report by the Department of Labour and National Service in February 1969 on 'Employment Opportunities in Domestic Service' commented:

> There is no evidence that female migrants find domestic work more attractive than do Australian-born women. (Department of Immigration File 69/72632)

However, under the Worker Requisition scheme, more women were accepted under the domestics category than any other 'female' occupation. Furthermore, their class was already anticipated, as the report suggests:

> The demand for private domestics is strongest in the major metropolitan centres, and more particularly in the middle and upper class suburbs. There is little demand for this type of worker from the poorer and working class suburbs although it is from these areas that come the majority of women seeking domestic employment.

In 1971, in response to the 'Balance of the Sexes' recommendation on female employment, it was reported that:

> During the post-Second World War period the incidence of unemployment in Australia has been higher among women than among men . . . And yet job opportunities, taken in the aggregate, have been more plentiful for females than for males . . .
>
> The problem of employment opportunities for women arises not because of an overall insufficiency of jobs but largely because of a mal-distribution of available jobs. In other words, job vacancies and job applicants are not as well 'matched' in the case of females as in the case of males. (Department of Immigration File 69/72632)

The writer expressed the view that the cause of this 'mal-distribution' was both an imbalance in the geographical location of labour demand and labour supply and a divergence between the skills of the job seekers and those required by the jobs. The report purported to address the recommendation made by the Committee on the Balance of the Sexes that the employment opportunities for women should be 'broader', yet it focused on ways to train women for those same limited occupations for which there was already a demand.

A working woman, it was assumed, would have only a few employment options and her ability, or willingness, to perform in those areas of employment was the only occupation-related criterion specified in 1971:

> Knowledge of English would be an advantage for clerical workers and secretaries but lack of English should not disqualify single women for assistance provided they are willing and able to take unskilled work e.g. in factories, domestic duties in hospitals, until they have sufficient knowledge of English for employers to be prepared to accept them for office duties.

At least as early as 1964 intending immigrants were showing an interest in employment opportunities for *married* women, as noted by one Chief Migration Officer (CMO) in London:

> Frequently selection officers are asked for advice as to the possibility of married women obtaining employment in particular areas in Australia and it has been suggested that we should endeavour to obtain a regular report ... from Australia giving us the up-to-date indications of the prospects of employment for married women. (Department of Immigration File 67/70369)

The 'gain' for Australia in married women immigrants working could be measured in its social rather than economic terms, according to the CMO, an opinion reflected in policy throughout the period:

> There is no need for me to elaborate on this particular question except to say that if a family composition is such that a mother is able to leave her children during the day and obtain employment, it must help immensely in many ways. There is, of course, the extra money coming into the household and the opportunity afforded to the wives to mix with Australians generally and this is, in our view, of paramount importance from an assimilation view point. (Department of Immigration File 67/70369)

This interest was just as real in Italy in the late 1960s as an immigration officer, discussing counselling of wives, recounts:

> Well why do you want to go to Australia? For work was the standard sort of an answer. Quite often they had heard that they could get a job, they'd heard through the grape vine what was available. All that was available for women (in the south of Italy) was dressmaking at home, sewing on sequins or rural work, vine harvest, olive harvest, not factory type work. (1969)

And more than a decade later, in Lebanon:

> I think by and large the better educated ones would have been looking for an opportunity to do work of one sort or another. Women from rural areas would have worked in the fields, cultivating crops and the like and invariably they would say they were not all that keen about working in Australia because they wanted to stay and look after the family. (1982)

In advising the Department on employment opportunities for single women immigrants, in response to the Balance of the Sexes recommendation, the Department of Labour and National Service noted two studies undertaken in 1970. One was on female unemployment in regional centres, which stated that 'a large percentage of the female unemployed are migrants' and the other was a 'Report of Analysis of Characteristics of Married Women Registered with the Commonwealth Employment Service at 10th April 1970'.

This showed that 62% of the unemployed married women registered for employment in South Australia were migrants in contrast to 30% in New South Wales. The report also revealed an increasing proportion of married women migrants seeking part-time employment. (Department of Immigration File 69/72632)

In writing policy and advising immigration officers, however, policy-makers seem to have based their idea of the Australian norm, not on prevailing figures, but on an old-fashioned notion of the role of the Australian woman. While the relevance of female labour to the Australian labour force or the importance of women's incomes to the Australian family is not acknowledged in the immigration programs, the reality of women's position vis à vis the work force was beginning to get recognition in bureaucratic circles in the 1970s.

It appears that while investigating the question of widening employment opportunities for women as a means of attracting single women immigrants, the findings of greater unemployment among women in general and married immigrant women in particular introduced this question as a settlement issue; as well, thereby, adding to the awakening consciousness within the Department that women were in the labour force. In a Minute to the Commonwealth Director of Migration, Adelaide, on 2 March 1970, the Secretary expressed a concern about BHP's recruitment of married male workers (because of the availability of accommodation for couples) for unskilled employment in their Whyalla steelworks:

We understand that there is a fairly serious shortage of female employment opportunities in Whyalla. The January figures for the Port Augusta Regional Employment Office show ten times as many registered female job seekers as there are vacancies for them. It seems likely that the company's decision to concentrate on recruiting married men will add to this problem ... Could you advise whether B.H.P. has any plans to increase the number of jobs available to women and whether you envisage any other developments which would help to alleviate the present scarcity of female employment. (Department of Immigration File 69/72632)

In 1973 three issues conspired to force the Department to rethink its policy on single women. The first was an argued balancing of the sexes brought about by the policies of the previous decade; the second was the abolition of the 'White Australia Policy' and the third was the acknowledgment that married women worked. In July 1973 the policy on single women was modified to require that single women immigrants be 'economically viable'. In a policy advice notice, it was explained that:

If Australia continues to experience a high rate of entry to the labour force by married women, this will produce a steady increase of female labour which might otherwise have been provided by migration of single females . . . any move to accept an increased number of single girls will have to be carefully considered to take account simultaneously of their marriage prospects, their ability to be absorbed into the labour force, and their integration potential. Admitting them outside these joint criteria . . . could also be prejudicial to the interests of Australia in producing an inflow of female labour incapable of being absorbed fully into the labour force and possessing limited marriage prospects. It could also lead to the establishment of ethnic communities not currently present in Australia with backgrounds which preclude their ready integration.

So, coinciding with the introduction of a non-discriminatory policy (on grounds of race), single women were no longer 'in the national need' after fourteen years of liberal provisions for their entry and only four years after a special committee was set up to look into ways of encouraging their immigration. An immigrant who had no literacy, educational or occupational prerequisites could come from anywhere and sponsor all sorts of 'unwanted immigrants' through the family reunion program. As single women had no such requirements, it would appear that they were perceived by elements in the Department as a potential source of unwanted immigration under the new non-discriminatory policy. It should be noted that the statistics used to assess whether there was still an imbalance in the sexes in the above report relied on the age groups 15–34 for females and 20–39 for males. The age groups on which the original policy was based were 16–30 for females and 18–35 for males. Overseas offices were advised that single women's employment prospects should be considered and that nurses and clerical workers would need to speak English and finally:

As far as the other employment avenues are concerned it can be expected that further supply of women to work in factories and as domestic servants, etc., will be forthcoming from the continuously increasing work participation of married females in Australia and from traditional source countries. (Department of Immigration File 69/71003)

Thus ended the period of liberal entry for single women immigrants, squeezed out by entrenched views of racial desirability and competition with married women for the narrow employment fields. Again the only means of immigrant entry for a woman was through her relationship with a male immigrant, as a dependant or with sponsorship and a maintenance guarantee.

Women and skill

After the early 1970s, the criterion of 'skill' assumed prominence in Australian immigrant selection processes. Weight was variously given to level of education and occupation in assessing skill. Again, women were marginalised in that they were not recognised as having skills that characterised the ideal immigrant. For skill, in Australia, has been constructed historically as a property of males. Certain tasks and jobs are seen to require 'skill'. Viewed as skilled individuals, men who have been disproportionately employed in those occupations have accrued political power over what has subsequently been defined as 'skilled' (Bennett 1984). Assessment of 'skill' has therefore been based on occupations that people have had rather than the competencies of people themselves.

The 1982 Migrant Entry Handbook, at item 20.4.4, indicates how 'points [determining immigrant selection in the independent and concessional family categories] are awarded according to the skill level of an applicant as determined by his worker code'; ten factors, including skill but also age, education, English ability and occupational attributes, were used to rank a prospective immigrant and the 'pass' score at the time was 60 or more points. The points awarded for 'skill' were given according to occupational designations, as follows:

Professional and technical	10 points
Skilled (specified worker codes)	10 points
Professional, technical and skilled workers whose qualifications are not fully recognised	6 points
Service occupations	4 points
Clerical, commercial and administrative	3 points
Semi-skilled	2 points
Rural	0 points
Unskilled	0 points

At particular times, particular 'skills' were designated as in 'occupational demand' in the Australian labour market—28 points could be awarded an immigrant intending to work in an occupation in 'shortage' and 24 if intending to work in an area of 'minor shortage'. Business immigrants and employment nominees were always classified as in shortage—thus business immigrants (usually men) would accrue more points than those in the 'clerical, commercial and administrative' designation (often women) of the above list. A further 10 points were available if the applicant had 'outstanding occupational attributes'; to accrue these points, the 1982 manual indicates:

an applicant would normally show all of the following attributes:

- several years experience in employment in the occupation in which he proposes to work in Australia

- a past record of employment which shows a stable, responsible approach to employment and a record of success and achievement

- good progress in his past career, where the occupation is one in which career advancement is possible

- personal qualities relevant to the proposed employment in Australia; these could vary widely from case to case eg for an applicant in a manual occupation involving heavy lifting they would include size and strength; for an applicant in a managerial occupation, they might include responsiveness, initiative and appearance. (Item 20.4.24)

Now, clearly this material did not exclude women who satisfied the criteria. However, if the criteria are examined, it is also clear that women as a general rule fitted the requirements far less frequently than men. With regard to points for 'skill' allocated to those with experience in certain occupations, the unskilled category included domestic work or house duties in which women were often occupied. And the lowly rated service sector or clerical, administrative and semi-skilled tasks included many of the jobs in which women worked in the paid labour force. (We noted already that business immigrants, disproportionately men, received extra points for being 'in shortage', that workers from commercial backgrounds did not get.) The 'outstanding occupational attributes' points were also unlikely to go to women, women being less likely to have completed continuous service in career-advancing jobs because of absences from the work force due to child rearing. Furthermore, they were more likely to be in jobs without prospects of career advancement. And if women applicants were expected to fit, with their personal qualities and aspirations, into the labour market for women in Australia, then they had to be defined in terms of Australia's highly sex-segregated labour market. This located them right in the category of worker least likely to generate points for skill in immigration selection. The difficulties for women to gain entry under these categories encouraged them to apply through the Preferential Family/Dependent Spouse categories, even if they had intended otherwise.

The points test on which selection of Independent and Concessional Family immigrants is based has continued to stress skill. In 1989, for instance, the preferred occupational and education characteristics could net the applicant far more points than any other item (like family relationship, age or language skills). This remains the case in 1993.

We have referred already to the coincidence of the Immigration Department's consideration of paid employment for women immigrants, and their efforts to attract single women to Australia. This reflects a concern with the 'gender balance' of the immigrant population—itself a product of the program's masculinist focus previously. The question of gender balance was important in immigration policy-thinking in the 1960s and deserves a separate mention.

Gender balance

By the early 1960s the Department had become aware of an 'imbalance in the sexes' among the immigrant population. In 1956, however, the Australian immigrant population within 'marriageable age' (that is, 18–35 for men and 16–30 for women) had had 136 men to every 100 females (Department of Immigration File 65/46611). In the mid-1960s, Hubert Opperman, the then Minister for Immigration, travelled to Europe to institute the immigration of young single females who would redress the imbalance. As he wrote in 1966:

the problem of how to encourage a larger proportion of single women to come to Australia was well to the forefront of my thinking during my overseas visit in 1965. (Department of Immigration File 65/46611)

The manuals reveal (as we have noted) that these women had to be of 'marriageable age', they need not have an occupation, were to be given assisted passage and were to be housed, on arrival in Australia, in separate hostels. Programs to educate young Greek women in Australian domestic techniques under a 'Women's Vocational Training Programme' were set up in Athens to produce domestics and useful wives for Greek husbands. By the early 1970s, immigrant men who had travelled to Australia without their families or who had arrived single and become engaged to women overseas, were able to bring them out under the assisted passage scheme, whether or not they themselves had been eligible for assisted passage. The 'Bring Back a Bride Scheme' of the 1970s went so far as to pay a return passage for immigrant men going back to their country of origin to find a wife.

Moral issues were discussed because of the perceived dangers of introducing single women to the immigration program. The 1969 report on the Balance of the Sexes pointed out that:

A basic problem in any programme for the migration of single women other than as members of a family group or on the sponsorship of close relatives is that of providing living accommodation under conditions that ensure their moral welfare. (Department of Immigration File 69/70582)

In a draft report on 'Accommodation for Single Women' of 24 December 1969 it was written:

there are special problems of supervision (in the moral sense) for Yugoslav, Spanish and Italian girls and to a lesser extent for Greek girls, because their countrymen tend to try to take advantage of their ignorance of language, customs, etc. in the early period after their arrival. (Department of Immigration File 69/71003)

This settlement policy of providing separate accommodation for single women was interpreted by one immigration officer thus: 'Otherwise you would have had an enterprising female running a brothel in one of our hostels' (1968).

In 1970, the case of a pregnant single woman who arrived in Australia under the Assisted Passage scheme was raised as an example of the possible abuse of that scheme in order to bring in men, the presumed fathers, who would not otherwise be accepted for immigration. In a report to the Assistant Secretary of the Operations Branch in November 1970, a senior officer commented:

I do think that there is a strong possibility that processing at our overseas posts might tend to the Victorian idea that female applicants fall into two categories only—the married woman who might possibly be pregnant and the single woman who could not possibly be pregnant.

In our present state of society this is not good enough and I think that we must face up to the fact that single women applying to us for assisted unaccompanied movement to Australia could well be pregnant.

All criteria designed to restrict or control entry of immigrants had been lifted in relation to single women from 1959 in order to facilitate the entry of as many as possible. A 1964 manual stated:

Unmarried females between 18 and 35 years of age will be considered for admission irrespective of their occupation.

The 1959 manual advises officers that while male fiancés nominated by Australian women are given only temporary entry and require a bond to be lodged on their behalf, female fiancées are given permanent entry on arrival, are not checked to ensure their marriage takes place and are not bonded:

Nominations for the entry of fiancées may be approved . . . provided the officer is satisfied that the application is bona fide. (Bonds need no longer be obtained.)

No follow-up action is necessary to ascertain whether or not the nominee married her sponsor after arrival. Fiancées are NOT landed under restriction (i.e. issued with temporary entry permits) . . .

The purpose of the looser criteria was to bring in women who were single and of marriageable age, as this advice from a 1964 handbook shows:

Where an application for the admission of a woman has been approved on the condition that she should arrive in Australia as a single woman . . . and it transpires that she is married, a visa should be refused.

No barrier was to stand in the way of single women or the wives or fiancées of immigrants and Australian residents entering Australia. In 1964 the literacy test was required of everyone except:

(i)   wives, minor unmarried children and dependent parents of residents of Australia;
(ii) fiancées of residents of Australia;
(iii) wives and minor unmarried children of immigrants who have themselves passed the test;
(iv) single women of any age.

And:

admission of a wife and/or minor children should not be refused because they are below Australian standards from the point of view of cleanliness or hygiene.

In 1971 age limits were relaxed for some women:

No specific upper age limits are laid down for unmarried women in Italy or Yugoslavia or nominated . . .

And in 1972:

the 'proxy' wife of a resident of Australia is to be given the same consideration, for immigration purposes, as any other wife.

The 'balance of the sexes' issue, the difficulties of overcoming the imbalance and the purpose behind the relaxed policy governing immigration of single women were clearly illustrated in this letter by the then Minister for Immigration, B. M. Snedden, in November 1967:

> Unfortunately, the recruitment abroad of single women meets its greatest obstacle in their reluctance to migrate or their families' objection to their migration. These obstacles are unlikely to be overcome by Government action, however well intentioned. Paradoxically enough, the surplus of marriageable males, which is a characteristic of all countries of immigration, is the most potent factor in attracting young nubile women either as fiancées or proxy brides, or as young wives acquired by migrants visiting their home countries.

In a further measure to facilitate the entry of single women, the Departmental Secretary recommended to the Minister, in 1968, that Eastern European sponsors should not have to meet the 'personal knowledge' criteria before nominating a fiancée for immigration, as many made contact through magazine advertisements and correspondence clubs:

> I think that we must question whether our real need to facilitate the admission of single girls from 'Operation Re-Union' countries is not such as to make acceptance of the security risk involved necessary. (Department of Immigration File 69/70582)

In 11 May 1969 the Minister announced an extension of the assisted migration program for single women from Greece. They could now be sponsored by 'relatives up to the degree of second cousins'.

Women, generally, were expected to be sponsored to Australia by their husbands or fiancés or by a male relative already resident who could give 'maintenance guarantees' that he would support her and any children. If married, the women were not to come without their husbands; if with children, they were not to be given assisted passage or subsidised accommodation; if single, they were not to be housed with other immigrants. The woman without a man to maintain or support her was a 'special breed' according to the 1971 handbook:

> Unmarried women may be considered as unsponsored migrants irrespective of occupation provided they appear to be self-reliant and capable of fending for themselves in a new country . . . However, women who have had no employment experience outside the home would not usually be acceptable as unsponsored migrants.

An immigration officer recalls an example:

> I just remember there was one Irish woman came through there. She'd worked, she was capable of doing semi-skilled work, she was prepared to accept any work in Australia, she met health and character requirements. Those, you had to exercise a bit of judgment—whether they were likely to hold down a job, or obtain a job—because we usually relied on the sponsor providing assistance. (1970)

There is little doubt that the push to introduce greater numbers of single women into Australia was for the purpose of presenting

Australia's masculine population with a pool of potential wives, hence the emphasis on the women's marriageability. Of the possibility that Australian women might sponsor fiancés from overseas, one immigration officer reflected that:

> We were encouraging females to come into this country, there was an imbalance here amongst the migrants, to marry off the males in this country. We didn't want Australian women wanting to bring in *workers* from outside. (1970, our emphasis)

Marriageability seemed to be the only criterion under some programs. For a short period in 1972, a debate was sparked in the Federal Parliament and in the media around this issue, by a statement by the then Shadow Minister for Immigration, Mr Grassby, in Parliament on 18 May 1972, in which he said:

> in the past year or so nearly 2,000 of the flower of South American single womanhood have come to Sydney and Melbourne . . . well educated and well raised senoritas have come from Peru . . . It is the opinion of the girls themselves that the Australian Government has brought them to this country as marriage fodder . . . (Department of Immigration File 72/76644)

This statement was refuted by the Department by pointing to the fact that slightly greater numbers of South American single men had immigrated during the same period and the Immigration Office in Peru reported that:

> at no stage did the Embassy 'recruit' large numbers of single girls let alone encourage them to migrate with a view of ready matrimony in Australia. The girls apply voluntarily and do so in large numbers. Statistically, neither Australia nor Peru have an imbalance between the sexes to speak of . . .

It would appear that the Department was attempting to engineer the social make-up of Australia's immigrant intake with particular emphasis on economic and occupational characteristics in relation to male immigrants and marriageability characteristics in relation to female immigrants. At the same time the Department was sensitive to accusations of using female immigrants as 'marriage fodder'. Since the upper age criterion for women was brought into line with that for men, in 1976, the emphasis on single marriageable women as immigrants has declined.

Consciousness of gender issues within the bureaucracy

As was noted in the introduction to this chapter, claims that the Immigration Department was somehow prejudiced in its view of immigrant women may certainly not be made in hindsight, based only on applying the standards of today's policy discourses to the past. Though some of the past practices and policies about immigrant men and women appear sexist, when viewed from a contemporary vantage point, this section indicates how a consciousness of the gender biases of immigration policy was starting to stir in the Immigration Department bureaucracy in the 1970s, and was certainly apparent from the mid-1980s. Further, there is some evidence that the Immigration Department was one of the group of reasonably progressive federal departments in this regard.

Comparing the 'gender consciousness' of the Immigration Department with that of the federal Department of Employment (known presently as the Department of Employment, Education and Training, or DEET), several points can be made.

The first point is that if we compare the positions taken by the Departmental Women's Co-Ordinator and later the Women's Desk of the Department of Immigration with its counterpart (the very important Women's Bureau in the Department of Employment), there seems no ground to claim that the Immigration Department's thinking on gender issues among those concerned with those issues lagged behind that of the Women's Bureau. Evidence of an exchange of correspondence and views between the Department of Immigration staff and the newly appointed head of the Women's Bureau is in Department of Immigration File 83/76479 and it shows the immigration staffperson briefing the new Director on research and community issues to do with immigrant women. It then records their agreement to look into the possibility of joint research projects.

The question of the relative progressiveness on women's issues of these federal departments as a whole (a second point) is another issue. One statement made in Parliament by the Leader of the Opposition on 28 November 1985 (and recorded in Hansard, p. 3914) indicates that under the Fraser Government (1975–82) 'there was the establishment of a special women's unit with the Department of Education, the Department of Social Security, the Attorney-General's Department, the Schools Commission and the Australian Development Assistance Bureau'. The Department of Immigration is missing from this list—it had a Women's Co-ordinator in its Ethnic Affairs Branch by mid-1983, but not a women's unit; in fact, the position of Women's Co-ordinator had been 'recently re-established' in mid-1983 (see Department of Immigration File 83/76479, folio 9), indicating that, in some of the Fraser years, there was no dedicated women's issues body in the Immigration portfolio. This re-establishment of the position of Women's Co-ordinator in early 1983 was seen as the 'first step towards creating the Women's Desk proposed in the ALP policy statement on migrant women' (Department of Immigration File 83/76479, folio 9). The early task of the Women's Co-ordinator was to compile a bibliography on immigrant women; meetings with community organisations were also being held by the Co-ordinator, especially those organisations concerned with women in industrial work. It appears that the Immigration Department responded to the new ALP Government's requirement for a Women's Desk in 1983 but was slower than some other departments in its action on this issue because it did not create what the previous Prime Minister had asked for.

Neither is it clear that the Women's Bureau was a part of the DEET bureaucracy (as it was called in 1992, or Department of Employment and Industrial Relations as it was called in 1984) that always sided with or was supported by its host department. A newspaper report (*Financial Review*, 20 September 1984, p. 10) reported that 'the Women's Bureau in the Department of Employment and Industrial Relations has differed substantially from the department in recommending a major restructuring of Federal Government employment and training programs which it claims have discriminated against females'. An article in the same newspaper (7 May 1992, p. 550) reported that the 28-year-old Women's Bureau was to be dismantled, reduced in staff numbers and 'its status will be downgraded from being a specialist branch to a unit in a new wider branch nominally called the Women's Policy, Income Support and Participation Branch'.

Third, it is not clear how much the views of the Women's Coordinator or Desk in the Immigration Department actually affected the design of settlement policy and immigration selection criteria. (In the case of the Women's Bureau, its role as a special and separate Bureau enabled it to mount quite successful campaigns about women and work, and to shift these topics into public as well as policy debate —the significance for this task of the fact that the Australian women's movement was also focusing on these issues throughout the 1970s and 1980s cannot be underestimated.) In the mid-1970s, the Immigration Department's Working Party on Women's Affairs (set up after Prime Minister Fraser's request in 1976 that every department should have a body investigating women's affairs) devised a quite progressive charter, listing as its priorities 'the monitoring of selection criteria and procedures to ensure that there is no discrimination against potential immigrants on the basis of sex, and the examination of post-arrival needs of immigrants, in the light of the principle that immigrant women should not be disadvantaged in comparison with Australian-born women' (Department of Immigration File 76/76327). It was perhaps an ominous sign that the senior bureaucrat advising the Departmental Secretary of the decision to set up the Working Party in response to the Prime Minister's request for action on women's issues, ended his letter with the following:

> The real task of such Committees should be to work themselves out of existence in the shortest possible time. I would envisage the Committee reporting within three months, outlining the major problems to be pursued and perhaps coming up with some tentative solutions to these problems. (Department of Immigration File 76/76327, letter of 9 August 1976)

The same letter also emphasised that 'the special concerns of migrant women also relate to their husbands, children and other relatives. It is necessary, therefore, to look at the problems of migrant women in a community and family context'.

The view of the senior departmental bureaucrat in charge of the Working Party and its future, who saw the women's issue as able to be dealt with quickly and as involving at least some focus on the family and the community (the subsumed woman, rather than women as individuals), is readily contrasted with the list of principles and actions decided on by the committee once it met. The principles the committee decided to adopt are referred to above, and an action focus was to be taken on pre-embarkation counselling, discrimination in employment, child care, contact with other departments on women's issues, and selection assessment forms. Not a mention was made of women being primarily members of families.

Perhaps the senior bureaucrat in question was reflecting the federal government's emphasis on family reunion in immigration at that time, and also the work of previous departmental committees on selection criteria (which were indeed examined by the Working Party). An earlier report on immigration selection options included in File 76/76327 as something perused by the Working Party appears to have concluded that it was unnecessary to isolate women's issues in immigration selection. The principles which guided its deliberations made no reference to gender. They were '(1) that any system of migrant selection including the selection criteria, should be applied universally to all migrant applicants' and '(2) that the emphasis in immigration policy and hence migrant selection should be the welfare and settlement prospects of the individual migrant. Whilst manpower policy objectives are important, they should not be the dominant consideration in selection' (Department of Immigration File 76/76327). (This statement of the Liberal/National Party Coalition stands against the trajectory of immigrant selection thinking as one of the few (relatively short) times in which family issues were stressed above skill and occupational issues.) The findings of the committee go on to consider family concerns in immigration selection, rather than gender concerns or the interests of women.

While the Women's Bureau of the Department of Employment had been building up a profile in issues associated with women as paid workers, then, struggling within its own department to do so, the Department of Immigration in the 1970s was also undergoing some internal conflict over the depiction of women in the immigration process. Of course, the fact that the Australian women's movement focused on issues of women in the paid workplace during the 1970s and 1980s, but far less on immigrant-women-related matters like selection and settlement, would have made it harder for women activists within the Immigration Department to alter their Department's stances and actions.

Fourth, through the middle 1980s, the degree to which Women's Desks were incorporated at the core of departmental decision-making, or marginalised, varied between departments. The Government directed in 1984 and again in 1985 that all public sector agencies should have women's units or mechanisms to promote the Government's policies on the status of women. At the start of 1987, the Department of Immigration was one of only six departments to have full-time Women's Desk officers; nineteen departments then had part-time mechanisms. The Department of Immigration had considerable input to the Federal Government's first 'National Agenda for Women', released in 1988 and prepared by the Federal Government's Office for the Status of Women. The Immigration Department had been asked by the 1987 Secretaries Task Force on the Status of Women to convene and chair a working group on women from non-English-speaking backgrounds; its input to the National Agenda came from the work of this group. According to specifications for the input given by the Office of the Status of Women, but also the views of the working party, the input focused on the particular needs of NESB women to have access to all government services and to be treated equitably by them. In particular, the single greatest need of these women was to improve their English language skills and therefore their capacity to communicate.

Following this, the Immigration Department issued a Women's Issues Plan in 1991 to implement its commitments to immigrant women in the National Agenda. The Women's Issues section of the Department has, in developing this plan, been careful to identify goals from the Department's overall corporate plan, and translate these into practical outcomes to be expected for women. It also stresses the fact that the Prime Minister has directed that

> line managers rather than women's units were to be made responsible for implementing the Government's status of women policy. This means that all senior staff of the Department, from section heads in regional offices to the members of the Executive should commit themselves to undertaking the strategies of this workplan wherever they relate to their area of responsibility. (DILGEA 1991d, Women's Issues Plan, p. 5)

Presumably this bureaucratic move is to ensure that women's issues are not marginalised by being separated out in women's units to which no 'mainstream' attention is paid at all.

If the question is to be answered, then, of how similar the Department of Immigration has been to other federal departments in its consideration of women's issues, it could be hypothesised that it has gone further than many in establishing the bureaucratic trappings of gender awareness, as the Departmental Secretary recently stated (Conybeare 1992). This, perhaps, was only to be expected of a department with a major female client group and a large female staff. Most of the Department's activities in settlement and ethnic affairs appear to include awareness of gender issues as well—this is clear from the

Government's original and recent National Agenda for Women in which the needs of NESB women in Australia are cited. Whether the selection mechanisms of immigration policy and the other branches of the Department are equally gender-sensitive is less obvious. (Easteal (1992), for example, has claimed that NESB women in custody are not well treated by the compliance sections of the Immigration bureaucracy.) Presumably other departments with large female client bases are similarly variable in their gender sensitivity.

Conclusion

This chapter has documented the ways that immigration selection in the post-Second World War decades has represented male and (particularly) female immigrants in ways that we would now identify as inaccurate and inequitable. In the first twenty-five years after the war, brawn seemed the characteristic most sought after by Australian selection officers overseas, and women entered Australia primarily as dependants, family members, and were certainly scrutinised as to their marital status. Following this, a period began in which 'skill' was highly valued in immigrant selection; but again, we have argued, what women do has been valued less, for the attributes and experiences of men have been assessed the more valuable. We now, in Australia, have an immigration selection regime which is viewed by its architects and implementers as 'gender-neutral'. Is this, then, sufficient for achieving gender equity in immigrant selection, a situation in which prospective immigrant women fare as well as prospective immigrant men? Without pre-empting the material presented in chapter 5 we will conclude with the following comments.

When the current set of immigrant selection practices, with all its gender neutrality, is examined, it can be found still to rest either on definitions and understandings of skill that are gender-biased, or on the expectation that women will enter Australia as dependent family members. The 'skill' criteria predominate in the economic or skill entry categories; the 'family member' or 'marital status' criteria predominate in entry under family immigration. That women's skills are not valued highly is reflected, we propose, in the fact that so few women (compared with men) enter Australia under the categories emphasising skill and that so many women enter under the family reunion provisions. Does this matter? We argue that the relative exclusion of women from skills-based entry (reflecting, as it does, sexist views of who is skilled and why) is significant. Particularly, it would be significant if entry under marital and family status criteria were reduced. Then, the numbers of women entering Australia as immigrants would drop drastically. In any case, we regard it as a matter of gender inequity that men and women enter Australia as immigrants even if in approximately equal numbers overall, when this rests on inappropriate views of women's skills and on the application of rules about family status that rely heavily on women's marital circumstances.

Chapter 3 takes further the close links between immigrant status and marital status, which underpin the immigration of most women.

Chapter 3: Marriage and immigration status—inequitable for women?

This chapter focuses on the close links for many women migrating as permanent settlers to Australia between their marital status and their immigration status, consequent upon the state's use of marital status to regulate the flows of immigration by those deemed 'unskilled'. We have argued, in chapter 2, that the 'ideal immigrant', intentionally or not, has been and remains male because males best fit the selection criteria of physical capacity or skill. The inclusion of women in post-Second World War Australian immigration programs has, we propose, been primarily due to their legal (marital) status with regard to immigrating men. This has implications for gender equity, in that those women who cannot, or do not wish to, comply with policy expectations of their marital status, and who cannot gain immigration entry because of their skills or refugee status, may miss out. There is good reason for policy-makers to examine the need for women's immigration to be so tied to their marital status, and to consider whether they might be more equitably treated if this were not the case.

The Australian state is not alone in regulating immigration, in part, through criteria related to marital status. Indeed, internal migration within many countries, as well as migration between countries, is attributed importantly to marriage, as a facilitator of social and geographic mobility (Thadani & Todaro 1978). It may well be the case in Australia that the relative ease of married women's immigration is associated with a perception in government that immigrant women *are* primarily the dependants of men—a kind of policy-induced, self-fulfilling prophecy. Certainly, married women, as a general rule, immigrate to Australia with greater ease than other women.

Who are these 'other' categories of women, for whom immigration to Australia is more difficult? Hugo (1990, p. 47) points out that women may find their immigrant entry constrained if they are in extended family structures, consensual or common law marriages, if they are female heads of household, or if they are in a homosexual partnership. For women applying for immigrant entry to Australia through selection categories other than those based on skill, then, marital status other than that within a legally celebrated hetero-sexual, nuclear family is likely to cause difficulties, or at least to be viewed as problematic. Australia does not now have an immigration program that selects single women for entry—unlike, for example, Canada and its program recruiting domestic labourers, who are often women entering singly, from Caribbean countries. (During the 1960s, as we saw in chapter 2, Australia did set out to find single women and to make domestic workers of some of them.) There is no reason to think, however, that Australia is different from other countries in that more of its *illegal* immigrants are single women than married women (Simon & Brettell 1986, p. 7). Single women have a harder time immigrating legally, if deemed unskilled, than married women. They are more likely, then, to have to consider illegal entry as an immigration option.

For women of different marital characteristics, immigration to Australia (and indeed to other countries) may be more or less easy. The Australian state, as we will see later in this chapter, plays an important role in regulating this situation—by accepting certain sorts of marriages and not others as grounds for immigrant entry, by not facilitating the legal immigration of 'unskilled' single women, and so on. We note, however, that Australia has avoided distinguishing spouse immigration as a *human right* presumably because, under some circumstances, spouses are refused entry. For example, refusal may occur if a spouse fails to meet health or character criteria. Indeed, immigration handbooks have referred to the 'family reunion principle' to underline the purpose of the family reunion, including spouse entry provisions (see JSCMR 1991, pp. 33-4). A detailed international review of this question would highlight variations in the actions of national governments with respect to the marital status of women immigrants. In those countries which seek foreign labour on a temporary basis, being married and expecting to be accompanied by one's family may be a disadvantage for immigrant entry. The proactive role of the Philippines Government in facilitating the emi-gration of its single women to take up employment as contract domestic labourers in a range of Asian countries is of particular interest (see Lycklama 1989).

This chapter now presents, as a background, information on the legal definitions of marriage currently used by the Australian state in the selection of immigrants, and data on the numbers of immigrants entering Australia by virtue of their marital status. Then, a number of 'marriage-related scenarios' are presented, identifying some of the different ways in which women migrating to Australia come to rely on their marital status. These scenarios include: people entering as would be 'normally' envisaged under the Preferential Family category (that is, primarily wives joining husbands and vice versa); Australian residents travelling overseas to find a husband or wife; and illegal sham marriages. Based on these scenarios, a discussion will follow of the implications for gender equity of the reliance on marriage for immigrant selection.

Marriage as grounds for immigration

The interest of the state in the marital status of its citizens is the subject of specific legislation and regulation. It is not surprising, then, that the marital status of *prospective* citizens is similarly an interest of the state and is built into immigration regulations. The state's intervention is based on both pragmatic and philosophical (or ideological) grounds. The pragmatic concerns are bound up in the population-building orientation of the (permanent) immigration program. Australia has always had an emphasis on settlers and hence has encouraged family immigration and the immigration of persons in the prime ages for work and family formation. The philosophical or ideological grounds are beliefs that individual immigrants *in families* are crucial to settlement success and immigrants' contribution to Australia. Individual immigrants separate from their families are themselves less happy in settlement, and therefore offer less. The important point to note in this quite generous view of immigrants' best prospects is that it has rested on a particular understanding of women's status in immigrant families.

Given Australia's success in attracting immigrant applications, selection has been a fundamental characteristic of the state's role in immigration. Marital status has played an important part in the selection criteria, helping to associate migrating women with a particular status within the family unit. The whole panoply of legal definitions of marriage, non-marriage, dissolution of marriage and so on, as well as penalties and sanctions for associated illegal activities within and outside Australia, have been subject to state management and scrutiny. In effect, aspects of 'private' behaviour have become matters of 'public' regulation or policy.

Marriage-related definitions

Chapter 2 provided an historical perspective on immigration-related terms such as family unit, principal applicant and dependant. This section focuses on *contemporary* understandings of terms which are centred on marital status.

Everyday definitions of marriage are insufficient when decisions have to be made for purposes of selecting immigrants. The Procedures Advice Manuals (for example, 1989) of the Department of Immigration, Local Government and Ethnic Affairs (DILGEA, known since early 1993 as the Department of Immigration and Ethnic Affairs—DIEA) provide explicit definitions and other guidelines for the use of Departmental staff, to assist them to recognise marriages in terms of the *Migration Act* and Regulations, to assess whether marriages are 'genuine and continuing' and to address questions concerning the 'recognition of divorces and assessment of separation claims' (DILGEA 1989b, p. 1).

Conditions pertaining to marriage which are taken into account for immigration purposes are:

❑ existence of a genuine and continuing marriage;

❑ existence of a genuine single state; and

❑ existence of a state in which marriage is not currently intended.

The validity of marriage, non-marriage and related intentions is at issue in decisions for visa or entry permit in certain situations. These situations occur when a visa applicant is claiming eligibility based on: marriage to an Australian citizen or resident; being the spouse of the holder of, or principal applicant for, a visa/entry permit; or being free to marry, that is, a fiancé(e). Inclusion in an application as a dependent family-unit member rests also on current or imminent marital status.

There are specific definitions of *spouse* according to the *Migration Act* and Regulations. A spouse is a person:

❑ legally married to another person and the marriage is recognised by the *Migration Act* (and the marriage has not been ended by divorce, death or permanent separation); or

❑ in a recognised de facto relationship.

At the time of application for a visa or entry permit regarding the latter case, the persons must have lived together for the immediately preceding six months on a genuinely domestic basis and must not be of the same sex. *Marriage* and *family unit* are specified in considerable detail. Most marriages celebrated under the *Australian Marriage Act 1961* are recognised for the purposes of the *Migration Act*. Marriages recognised by local law in foreign countries are acceptable to the immigration authorities. Some marriages, although recognised in the countries where they are performed, are not acceptable for the purposes of the *Migration Act*. These include certain polygamous and under-age marriages, marriages between people within prohibited relationships and marriages where the consent is not 'real' consent. These same exclusions are found in the *Australian Marriage Act* itself.

A member of a family unit (a notion whose historical variations were referred to in chapter 2) refers to the following relationships:

❑ a spouse of an applicant;

❑ any dependent children of the applicant or the spouse of the applicant;

☐ any dependent children of such a dependent child; and

☐ certain dependent relatives of the applicant or his/her spouse who reside with them.

There is empirical evidence that the net effect of these definitions contributes to the feminisation of the immigrant inflow, because females are more likely to occupy many of these defined 'dependent' statuses.

Impact of the marriage category in statistical terms

Consider now the basic figures for marriage-related immigration in recent intakes. In the 1989-90 immigrant intake, 47 per cent of female settler arrivals and 44 per cent of male settler arrivals were married. At least 65.3 per cent of those women derived their eligibility to enter Australia from their marital status, by accompanying a Principal Applicant or by marrying an Australian resident or citizen. Including the numbers who entered as fiancées of Australian residents/citizens, an estimated 35.1 per cent of all female settler arrivals derived their immigration status directly through their marital status.

Regarding men, 42.7 per cent of all married men derived their eligibility to immigrate to Australia from their marital status. When fiancés are added, 21.4 per cent of all male settler arrivals met immigration requirements because they were the spouse of a Principal Applicant under one of the eligibility categories or because they were married or were engaged to an Australian resident or citizen. The disparity in these figures speaks for itself. From this one set of data, marriage-related immigration appears to be of great salience for women.

For total settler arrivals in the financial years 1988-1991, see table 3.1.

In 1990-91, 13 099 out of 43 155 settler arrivals entered Australia under the spouse component of the Preferential Family category. Of those, 3593 were accompanying dependants, leaving a total of 9506

Table 3.1: Settler arrivals by sex for financial years 1988–89, 1989–90, 1990–91

Sex	1988–89	1989–90	1990–91
Male	37 002	34 517	19 343
Female	52 146	37 825	28 812
Total	89 148	72 342	48 155

Source: BIPR Statistics Section—released for report in 1992.

who were the Principal Applicants and therefore were eligible for immigration because they were married to an Australian permanent resident or citizen. Of those, 6463 (68 per cent) were women. In 1989-90, from a total of 72 342 settlers, women accounted for 6605 (66.1 per cent) of a total 9987 Principal Applicant spouses and in 1988-89, from a total of 89 148 settlers, 6134 (65.2 per cent) of a total 9412 Principal Applicant spouses. In addition, in 1990-91, 3944 persons entered as fiancés of Australians; 2506 (63.5 per cent) were women. In 1989-90, 2722 (64.1 per cent) of a total 4246 were women; and in 1988-89 women numbered 2907 (66.8 per cent) of a total 4353. (See details in table 3.2.)

Combining the two categories, *spouse entry and fiancé entry* (table 3.2), a significant number of persons immigrate to Australia every year through marriage to an Australian resident or citizen. A total of 13 204 Principal Applicants and 3944 dependants arrived in these categories in 1990-91, 14 233 Principal Applicants and 3761 dependants in 1989-90 and 13 765 Principal Applicants and 3263 dependants in 1988-89. Approximately two-thirds of Principal Applicants and over half the dependants were female, demonstrating that marriage is a more significant justification for immigrant entry for women than it is for men.

On-shore applications by tourists and temporary residents to remain permanently in Australia on the basis that they have married, or are living in a de facto marital relationship with an Australian citizen or resident, accounted for an additional 7612 spouse cases, in 1990-91; 11 528 spouse cases in 1989-90; and 11 073 in 1988-89 (DILGEA 1992a; BIR 1991b; JSCMR 1991). These are referred to as change of status marriages. In 1989-90 and 1990-91, 14 033 of those cases were based on lawful marriages (not de facto marriages). In the 1989-90 period there was a total of 234 135 marriages that took place in Australia, making the ratio of change of status marriage cases to total marriages in Australia approximately 1:17 (ABS 1991a).

Thus, as a category for permanent entry into or stay in Australia, *spouse eligibility* has led to the entry of almost 30 000 persons, Principal Applicants and their dependants, per year in these recent years.

Continuing to use data from the ABS (1991a), it is evident that some 90 000 settler arrivals in the 1989-90 period (for example) entered under other categories. However, a very large proportion of these come as accompanying spouses of Principal Applicants. The Principal Applicants are eligible under various criteria in the Skill, Family, Humanitarian and Special components and bring with them even larger numbers of dependants, many of whom are spouses. In the 1989-90 period, in the Family, Skilled and Humanitarian components, 49 513 Principal Applicants brought with them 56 434 accompanying persons. Figures for the number of dependants or

Table 3.2: Settler arrivals by sex and visa category by Principal/accompanying showing spouse/fiancé categories, 1988–91

1988–89

	Spouse	Fiancé PA	Fiancé AM	Total
Male P/A	3 278	1348	98	4 724
Accompanying	1 405	179	4	1 588
Female P/A	6 134	2796	111	9 041
Accompanying	1 475	191	9	1 675
Total P/A	9 412	4144	209	13 765
Accompanying	2 880	370	13	3 263
Grand total	12 292	4514	222	17 028

1989–90

	Spouse	Fiancé PA	Fiancé AM	Total
Male P/A	3 382	1455	69	4 906
Accompanying	1 588	189	11	1 788
Female P/A	6 605	2571	151	9 327
Accompanying	1 734	228	11	1 973
Total P/A	9 987	4026	220	14 233
Accompanying	3 322	417	22	3 761
Grand total	13 309	4443	242	17 994

1990–91

	Spouse	Fiancé PA	Fiancé AM	Total
Male P/A	3 043[a]	1123[b]	69[b]	4 235
Accompanying	1 670[a]	178[b]	7[b]	1 855
Female P/A	6 463[c]	2329[d]	177[d]	8 969
Accompanying	1 923[c]	153[d]	13[d]	2 089
Total P/A	9 506	3452	246	13 204
Accompanying	3 593	331	20	3 944
Grand total	13 099	3783	266	17 148

Notes:
PA—Personally acquainted.
AM—Arranged marriage.
P/A Principal applicant

a. Not all permanent arrivals in 1990–91 had the three parts of their entry visas recorded. Without the dependency and statistical codes, the Statistics Section cannot identify whether the immigrant is a principal applicant or an accompanying family member. Therefore the category 'Not stated' has been split proportionately between P/A and Accompanying categories, based on the relative proportions of the previous two years, i.e. 68 per cent of the 1772 'not stated' have been included as P/As and the rest as Accompanying.

b. As for note a above. Of the 8386 'not stated' 79 per cent have been included as P/A and the rest as Accompanying.

c. Some figures are produced but only to the level of information available. Hence the Fiancé categories also include one category 'not further defined' (nfd). These have been split proportionately between PA and AM, based on the figures for the previous two years and then split proportionately between PA and Accompanying. Of the 623 'nfd' 94 per cent were allocated to Fiancé PA and of those 88.4 per cent were allocated to P/A. Six per cent were allocated to Fiancé AM and of those 95 per cent to P/A.

d. As for note c. Of 934, 95 per cent were allocated to Fiancé PA and of those 92 per cent to P/A. Of the 5 per cent allocated to Fiancé AM 93 per cent went to P/A.

Source: BIPR Statistics Division—released for report in 1992.

63

'accompanying persons' who are married are not available. By comparing the figures disaggregated by marital status with those disaggregated by Principal Applicant/Accompanying, however, it is possible to estimate that 40.5 per cent (21 437) of female settler arrivals in those three categories were accompanying their husbands or were married or engaged to Australians and that 25 per cent (12 914) of male settler arrivals were accompanying their wives or were married or engaged to Australians.

A striking difference between men and women exists in the Skill category. This emerges if we subtract the number of settlers under the age of 15 in the Skill category from the numbers 'accompanying' in that category (assuming first that all remaining females accompanying in that category are married and then assuming that they are all unmarried). If we use the equation for females and then for males, it is possible to estimate that from 35.3 per cent to 75.2 per cent of females were accompanying spouses, compared with 0 to 14.4 per cent of males.

These figures demonstrate that not only is marital status a very important factor in migratory practices but that it is of far greater significance for women than for men. Marital status is arguably a more influential characteristic for determining immigration outcomes for women than any other characteristic, such as education or occupation. Just why marriage should be more significant for women than for men is a question to which there is no simple answer. Based on our data, we offer certain speculations.

First, taking into consideration the approximate figures for the Skill Migration component, which show such an enormous difference for men and women, it is probable that the immigration assessment process and the sex-segregated nature of the Australian work force play some part. The Skill component includes a range of subcategories, one of which deals with those who were sponsored by an employer to fill a 'highly skilled' position. The definition of skill (as we have noted) in Australia is a masculine one and therefore male-dominated occupations qualify as 'highly skilled' more readily than female-dominated occupations. Furthermore, employers are often selecting an employee from an overseas, male-dominated market.

Secondly, we comment on the selection of Principal Applicants. In the categories of Independent and Concessional immigration, the assessing officer applies a points test to the Principal Applicant. The Principal Applicant is taken to be the person listed first in the application form. The applicant decides who to list first.

Often it is the husband or male 'head of family'; sometimes it is the person whose brother or sister sponsored the family, who may equally be the wife. In either case, should it be found that the Principal Applicant did not earn sufficient points to pass the points test, the assessing officer would then apply the same process to the spouse (if there is one). If the spouse meets the points test, he or she statistically becomes the Principal Applicant and the whole unit can immigrate, subject to other criteria (that is, health and character). As was seen in chapter 2, for the same reason that male occupations are more often regarded as 'highly skilled', male occupations attract more points than female occupations and therefore more men are likely to qualify for Skill immigration (and as Principal Applicants) than women. Furthermore, a similarly qualified or educated couple, had they listed the husband first, would be immigrating on the basis of his points test because there was no need for an assessing officer to test the wife. Statistically, then, the male would be the Principal Applicant and the wife an 'accompanying' dependant. This may lead to a lag in recognition of the woman's qualifications in Australia and, hence, to at least the likelihood of a period of unemployment or underemployment in Australia. It is also possible that in many couples the husband is better qualified than his wife. This seems to be borne out by the higher educational levels for males found in the Madden and Young study (1993b, p. 16).

It is somewhat paradoxical that the common practice of men marrying younger women sometimes means the wife earns more points for age than her husband and, all else being equal, both partners become eligible for immigration through her. This initial advantage does not seem to persist, however, on entry to the country of immigration. In most of the policy selection categories, the habit of applicants putting husband, father or male 'head of the family' on the application forms leads to men being considered as Principal Applicants and women as accompanying dependants. Humanitarian claims, on the other hand, may equally apply to every member of the family unit and therefore each would be independently eligible for immigration. In practice, however, the statistics do not reflect this possibility: as was noted in chapter 2, more males than females enter Australia under the refugee and humanitarian categories.

Typical scenarios relating marriage to immigration

In the previous section a marriage–immigration link was identified, through which twice as many women as men enter or stay in Australia each year. Government practices relating to nomination of one individual as Principal Applicant or as skilled person are some of the probable causes of this. There is a range of circumstances under which marriage immigration occurs, however, and the relationship of marriage to immigration has a distinctive nature in each. In this section, these differing circumstances will be explored in more detail by outlining a number of scenarios in which marriage and immigration go together, with women possibly disadvantaged by their linking.

In the first scenario, Australian citizens or permanent residents working or visiting overseas meet their partners, marry them or become engaged and then sponsor them as spouse or fiancé to immigrate to Australia. A typical example is the young Australian working holidaymaker in Britain. It is only a matter of chance that such a person met his or her partner in another country. It is their marriage that causes them to consider immigration, and the immigration provisions for spouses exist so that they can live together in one country.

> There were quite a lot of spouse sponsorships by Australian girls who'd gone on a working holiday who had met a friend in a pub and got into a relationship and wanted to bring them out, either married them or wanted to bring them out as a fiancé. (Immigration Officer, London, 1975)

A second scenario refers to overseas-born Australian residents. Like the single 'immigrant workers' of the past, the overseas-born person in Australia, contemplating marriage, returns to his or her place of origin with the express purpose of meeting a partner of the same ethnicity, culture, religion or language group, or to fulfil an arranged marriage obligation made years before. It is the Australian citizen's act of immigration in the first place that leads to the immigration of the spouse. Perhaps typical players in such scenarios are the Lebanon-born. Lebanese men who have immigrated at an earlier time return to Lebanon to find a wife; and young women, born in Australia to Lebanese parents or having immigrated to Australia with their parents as children, return to Lebanon with their parents to find a husband. Some of these marriages have been arranged by the families under traditional custom.

Interestingly, for many of the newly acquired spouses, immigration has a particular effect on the traditional family formation. Among many ethnic groups, women traditionally go to their husband's family after marriage. In the case of Australian Lebanese women, however, it is not uncommon that the women will sponsor their new Lebanese husbands to immigrate to Australia. Here the roles are reversed and the man joins his wife's family. Where immigration is a desirable goal and marriage brings with it an entitlement to immigrate, traditional practices may be forgone, suggesting that the relationship between marriage and immigration is a dynamic one.

> There were a lot of special concessions also for the Lebanese back in '75 and virtually whole villages just decamped and came to Australia. A lot of Shiite Muslims had come to Australia as adolescents or young men and had worked here, worked up a business or whatever and had gone back looking for a wife.

> And then we had females who had come to Australia as young girls and had been taken back by their parents to Lebanon to marry some person in their village who they may have recalled but invariably didn't know much about at all. (Immigration Officer, Beirut, 1983)

As a third scenario, men travel to countries (such as the Philippines or Thailand) with the express purpose of finding a wife. Alternatively, they use the services of a contact or agent to put them in touch with potential partners and invite them to visit Australia.

Studies of this practice suggest that both the Australian men and the women involved are operating in a tight marriage market in their own countries where, because of remoteness of location, social position, sex imbalance or age, their opportunities at home are limited. The primary purpose of both is to marry.

That they had to look for their spouse abroad brings both parties to confront immigration. In almost all cases, the women immigrate to Australia. Whether this is because their husbands' career and circumstances are considered more important and are located in Australia or because to both, living in Australia is a more desirable option than living in the other country, is not clear. However, as both seek certain positive characteristics in their potential partner, the prospect of immigration may be for the woman one of the attractions of the foreign male.

In status-conscious societies such as the Philippines, women of this background often have difficulties finding suitable husbands. Educated middle-class men often pass over them because of their provincial background. On the other hand, these women are reluctant to marry 'below' their standing in society, while lower-status men are reluctant to take wives 'above' theirs.

The desire of elder daughters to provide financial support for their families in the provinces increases the pressure on such women to 'marry well'—a pressure that has increased in the 1970s and 1980s as the Philippines economy has deteriorated. Agencies providing introductions to eligible men from an affluent country such as Australia offer one solution to such women. (Chuah et al. 1987)

Reunion provides a fourth scenario. As with the overseas-born who return to their country of origin to find a marriage partner, the overseas-born seeking to be reunited with their spouse and dependants is reminiscent of the practice of the immediate post-Second World War decades when men came to Australia without their families to save money and return home or to make a start and sponsor them later. Few immigrants would fall into this category now. Although the practice of sending one member of the family ahead to find a house or a job is not unknown, it is limited because a family unit must be processed together and is encouraged by the Australian authorities to travel together. However, many refugees find themselves in the position, after fleeing their country, perhaps spending time in a refugee camp and finally gaining entry to a third country of settlement, of having to sponsor their families because they had to leave them behind. This scenario is probably most common among the Vietnamese, who pool their resources to send an 'anchor' person (usually a male) who in turn sponsors the rest of the family when settled. For them, immigration facilitates their reunion in a more stable country.

A large percentage of the ones we were interviewing qualified under what is now called Preferential Family. They were immediate family, that is, wives and fiancés, parents or dependent children of people already in Australia. The sponsor was usually the male who comes out as the anchor. It's usually the man in his twenties to early thirties, or the eldest son of a family. The men were considered to be hardier in some ways and therefore it tended to be the male who was the sponsor, the husband or the son or the uncle or whatever. (Immigration Officer, Hanoi, 1989)

The last scenario is the reverse of the first, where temporary residents, tourists, working holidaymakers and students in Australia meet and marry an Australian resident or citizen, decide to live in Australia, and use the change of status provisions to apply for permanent residence. An example might be the young Malaysian students who, having spent several years completing their studies in Australia, have developed relationships with Australian residents or citizens. A second case is that of the UK, Canadian, Dutch and Japanese working holidaymakers who travel and work in Australia for up to a year. All fall within the highest 'age at marriage' category and have been in Australia a sufficient period of time to make romantic attachments. As marriage plays a role in the decision to immigrate, so may immigration play a role in the decision to marry. The temporary nature of a person's stay may force them into a decision to marry which might otherwise have been delayed or not taken place at all, had they been able to pursue a relationship with their partner at their own pace. This may also be true of the Australian visiting abroad, as in the first scenario. From the Madden and Young (1993a) study's transcripts about the decision to immigrate, of five UK-born women interviewed, two are reported to have come on a working holiday, during which they met and married their Australian husbands.

Examination of these scenarios provides some further suggestions as to why Australian immigration figures show more women entering in the marriage and fiancé categories than men.

In all, except perhaps the 'reunion' category, a couple must decide in which country they will reside after marriage. For many the decision may be based on economic considerations, which are more often tied up with male career and job opportunities. The wife's paid occupation (if she has one) is given secondary weighting. Therefore, more commonly, women migrate to their husband's chosen place of residence. For example:

[A Malaysian] student met and married her Malaysian husband while at university in Australia and although she 'still wanted to go home', the prospects of employment for her engineer husband were better in Australia and they applied for temporary then permanent migration. (Madden & Young 1993a)

The region from which immigrants are currently being drawn is likely to influence the numbers of women who will find it easier to enter Australia via marriage-related immigration. One example is the 'Filipino bride' phenomenon, already mentioned in the 'search for a partner overseas' scenario. This alone is responsible for the immigration of 1600 Filipino women as wives per year (Pendlebury 1990). Obviously numbers of this magnitude will contribute significantly to the larger proportion of women immigrating through marriage. Also, the region and circumstances from which immigrants have previously been drawn may affect subsequent migrations, as was clear in the scenario where Lebanese-Australians seek a partner from Lebanon. To the degree that those Australia-born travelling overseas to seek partners, under all our scenarios, are primarily men, then the statistics will reflect this in a higher incidence of women immigrating here for marriage.

All of the typical scenarios listed above, that link immigration to marriage very closely but in different ways, are legal and condoned by immigration authorities. Listing them helps to provide further reasons for the preponderance of women in those immigration flows to Australia that are marriage-generated. Is it clear that women are disadvantaged relative to men when they participate in immigration to Australia for these reasons? Our major response is that women are not disadvantaged by their participation in these flows, *so long as* these are not the only or primary means by which they may immigrate to Australia. That is, if immigrant selection criteria are such as often to preclude women from immigrating themselves, unless they are in the expected heterosexual, marital relationship, then we consider this to be of disadvantage to women, forcing them to rely on their marital status too much. Certainly, there will always be marriage-based, family reunion immigration to Australia, and for many women and men this is highly satisfactory and not a compromise of gender equity.

There are, however, two situations that should be stressed as likely producers of disadvantage for women immigrating to Australia. These are situations in which immigration is based on marriage. One was included in the list of scenarios above—the situation in which Australia-born men seek marriage partners overseas, but not because of ongoing cultural links with the country of origin of their families. Most often this situation occurs, as was noted, when Australia-born men seek Filipino women as their partners. In the next section we discuss this matter. In the following section the matter of sham marriages is discussed, along with its potential for disadvantaging women.

Filipino women as wives of Australian men

The issue of marriage in connection with female Filipino immigrants to Australia has achieved a certain notoriety because of the so-called 'Filipino brides' phenomenon, or 'mail-order bride' schemes. It is also a matter of demographics—the Philippines provides the highest proportion of women applicants for Australian spouse or fiancé visas based on cross-cultural relationships (DILGEA Minute, February 1991). Hence, the literature on Filipinos is more extensive than for other ethnic groups.

For example, 'Filipino Spouses' was the topic of an Immigration Department Minute in February 1989—an attempt by the Department to counter the adverse publicity which had been appearing regularly in the local press. (Other publications with similar purposes include *A Bride for All Reasons: Report on a Pilot Survey of Filipino Brides*, 1982; and Jackson and Flores' study, *No Filipinos in Manila: A Study of Filipino Migrants in Australia*, 1989.) The minute noted that 45 per cent of marriages between Filipinos and Australian citizens and residents occur in the Philippines and of the almost 10 500 Filipino immigrants in 1987–88, about 10 per cent arrived as spouses and 11 per cent as fiancées. As divorce is not recognised in the Philippines, de facto spouses applying for residence are not discriminated against by the Australian Government. The imbalance in the sexes among Filipino immigrants (that is, overwhelmingly in favour of women) has been redressed to some extent in recent years by the family reunion program, which has enabled the women to sponsor other members of their families.

More recent statistics indicate the growth of the Filipino population in Australia. For instance, Cahill (1990, pp. 20–1) reported that by June 1988 there were nearly 52 000 Philippines-born people in Australia (0.3 per cent of the total population); it was the twelfth-largest immigrant community; women outnumbered men 2.01:1 and, by 1988, the Philippines had become the third-largest source country for Australia's immigrants. The prime reasons for these trends are Filipino intermarriages, followed by the capacity this gives for sponsored chain migration. As Jackson and Flores (1989, p. 15) noted: 'there is no ethnic group of any comparable size in Australia which depends as much as do the Filipinos on the "family reunion" category of immigrants'.

Figures also show that the distribution of intermarriage between Filipinos and Australian males has been responsible for alleviating the lack of marriage opportunities for men in certain remote mining areas, especially in Northern Australia (Cahill 1990, p. 21).

To look at trends in the Philippines as well as in Australia, from the 1960s onwards female internal migration there has been very common and strongly economically based. This has been part of families' strategies to counter underemployment and poverty in rural areas. Among the consequences of population movements of this kind have been female concentrations in Filipino urban areas, a significant transfer of funds from urban to rural areas via remittances, and a marriage squeeze for females in urban settings. Migration to overseas destinations has also occurred as part of families' strategies to gain economic benefits from different sorts of migration. This emigration has been accompanied by a rise in intermarriages occurring within the Philippines and in countries of immigration.

The extent of inter-country marriage has caused concerns in the Philippines, one of which is that the operation of a marriage 'trade' has developed, which is not necessarily always advantageous to Filipinos. Carmichael (1988, p. 86), for example, said: 'recent migration of Filipino females to Australia has been tied to the marriage process itself, with the development of the commercially promoted traffic in Filipino brides'.

Other analysts have reported advantages for Filipino women in immigration:

> It is evident that [Filipino] women in migration do not perceive themselves, and do not wish to be seen, in the traditional light of primarily physical agents for reproduction. While not denying their child-bearing rights and capacity, and while not undermining the value of the family, (female) migrants manifest a clear appetite for a more diversified role leading to a greater space for self-determination and freer decision-making process: towards autonomy and transcendence. (Cruz & Paganoni 1989, p. 101)

It is our contention that positive interpretations of their marriage for immigration might describe the original intentions of many female immigrants. Those intentions, however, may become altered by the actual experience of permanent or temporary migration. This occurs both because of the circumstances surrounding the migration process (including immigration policy *per se* and its application by immigration personnel), but also the intentions and actions of foreign partners.

Along with legal issues such as marriage fraud and practical issues such as disadvantageous occupational placement or downward economic mobility, there are social–psychological aspects of marriage-driven immigration which may bear more heavily on women than men. Australian researchers have discussed these in the context of marriages between Filipino women and non-Filipino men, though they would apply in the case of other marriages. Cahill (1990), for example, has examined the phenomenon of intermarriage in relation to Filipino women and Japanese, Swiss and Australian partners. He also commented on some general aspects of intermarriage, particularly on reactions to it. He noted, that:

> the decision to marry outside one's own group more often than not generates considerable intellectual and emotional conflict. It may be perceived as a repudiation of one's own cultural, religious and/or linguistic heritage; it may be perceived as catastrophic in personal terms as it will surely lead to irretrievable marriage breakdown; it may be perceived as a contamination of the purity of racial stock or of an ethno-cultural or religious tradition. (p. 2)

Marital distance, the greater or lesser difference between participating partners based on variables such as class, caste, religious, ethnic, racial, linguistic or national difference, characterises Filipino marriages in Cahill's view. Given the concern over the breakdown rate of Filipino–Australian marriages, often with the occurrence of domestic violence, marital distance may be one of the contributing factors.

The disadvantages for women entering Australia in circumstances of intermarriage and marital distance relate to how they fare once here. Considerable effort has been made by the Association of Non-English-Speaking Background Women of Australia (ANESBWA) to enlist government support for immigrant women whose relationship or marriage to an Australian male breaks down once she is here. As the organisation's president describes:

> There are documented cases where women who arrived here as tourists or as fiancées and established a relationship with a partner from this country have been used and abused by the partner and subsequently abused by the system which has determined that her only right to stay in this country is on the grounds of an on-going relationship with an Australian resident or citizen ... In many of the cases with which I have had professional experience, it is part of the pattern that when the marriage/relationship breaks down before, and even after permanent residence is obtained, the male partner invariably informs the Department of Immigration that the marriage/relationship was one of convenience and a ruse for the woman to gain residence in Australia ... The essence of our argument has been that under the Act and Regulations, women who had married or entered into a defacto relationship with an Australian citizen or resident, and whose relationship had become violent, were being forced to remain in the relationship or else to leave Australia if they chose to escape the violence ... Many of the women also fear retribution and stigmatisation on returning to their country of origin ... the recurrent theme is that as a consequence of the Australian immigration legislation, women are being punished for the violent crimes of their partners ... Progress was made in April 1991, when Minister Hand introduced regulations 126 and 135m which have made some provision for victims of domestic violence ... There are however concerns even in these—the fact is that an application on spouse grounds requires a fee of $750.00 ... There is also only two year temporary entry permits given in this category ... ANESBWA asks why do the marriages of immigrants have to guarantee a success rate higher than that of the general community? Applicants for permanent residence on spouse grounds who leave their violent spouse, will now be considered for residence after they provide the Department with the required proof of this violence ... This proof consists of the applicant providing the Department with either a Domestic Violence Order ... against the partner, or else evidence of a proven charge of assault against the applicant by the Australian partner ... many women do not have access to legal information, some magistrates do not grant these orders, and in many cases the women fear retribution and further violence if they proceed with seeking these orders ... There is also a strong culture in the Department, in the Joint Select Committee and in some sectors of the community, which believes that most of these applications are fraudulent. (Mottee 1992)

In a submission to the Joint Standing Committee on Migration Regulations (JSCMR) (1991, pp. 79–80), it was emphasised that:

In most cases migrant women are detached from their families and support systems. Many of them lack English, knowledge about services and their legal rights. Even if they know about services, access is difficult or they show a high level of reticence to approaching these services. This vulnerability is aggravated by the immigration law which forces them to 'choose' between remaining in a 'marital' situation fraught by domestic violence or face deportation. It is this additional vulnerability which distinguishes immigrant women . . . the threat of deportation can be used as a tool of coercion, restricting a partner from leaving a relationship or seeking the protection of the law.

These submissions among others led to the progress made in April 1991, when the Immigration Minister introduced Regulations 126 and 135m in order to make some provision for the 'victims of domestic violence' referred to by Mottee. Provision was made for permanent resident status to be granted to persons who were the spouse of an Australian citizen or resident, had been in a genuine relationship but whose relationship had broken down due to domestic violence.

Another outcome of community and official concern over this issue is the *Serial Marriage Project* commissioned by the Women's Issues Section of the Department of Immigration, Canberra, and undertaken by Dr Robyn Iredale. The impetus for the study came from the Filipino community in Australia, members of which suggested that the current selection process which enables Australian men to sponsor Filipino women on the basis of marriage, is biased against the women. This is because only the Filipino applicant (not the sponsor, who is usually an Australian male) has to undergo health and character checks. As part of this complaint, the community provided anecdotal evidence that some Filipino women who had gained entry to Australia as immigrants because of marriage to an Australian citizen had been subjected to domestic violence and divorce, leaving the ex-husband free to return to the Philippines to sponsor another woman for marriage. This then becomes *serial sponsorship*.

Sham marriages—the 'unrespectable' side of marriage

It is due to the relative simplicity of the marriage category that it can be abused by persons whose aim is entry to Australia and who are able and willing to enter into a marriage for the sole purpose of circumventing other eligibility criteria. The JSCMR, in its report, *Change of Status: Marriage and De Facto Relationships* (1991, p. 53), explained:

> Marriage, including in Australia a de facto marriage, represents for many the only or the simplest way to qualify for migration or residence. Visitors, students or working holiday makers in Australia who want to make this

their home quickly realise that a marriage to an Australian citizen or resident can be their best route. In evidence to the Committee the Department described the de facto category in particular as 'an opportunity to write your own ticket'.

Such sham marriages are not uncommon and have, over the years, given rise to stricter policy guidelines and tighter procedures for assessment of the marriage. The test for whether a person may enter, or remain, as the spouse of an Australian resident or citizen is whether the marriage is a 'genuine and continuing' one. The JSCMR report (1991, pp. 54–5) explains how this approach differs from that taken in other countries such as Britain:

> In Britain the rules permitting spouses to enter and stay are seen as 'the Achilles heel' of strict immigration control. By proscribing sham marriages and those contracted for a 'primary' immigration purpose authorities intend to curb abuse and 'protect the labour market'. In Australia the rule is not designed specifically to cut down the numbers of spouse applicants, but rather to ensure that qualifying spouses are genuinely entering for the purpose stated, namely to live with their Australian partners.

As a Department of Immigration officer stated in evidence to the Committee:

> In a sense, we do not really care or investigate what their motives are, whether for love or money or if part of the reason for the marriage is to gain entry to Australia, provided the intention is to enter into a genuine and ongoing relationship. It is a matter of the intention of the parties to enter into a genuine and ongoing relationship . . . That is what the criteria seek to address.

This test also applies to de facto marriages. While making the process of entry as a spouse more demanding on genuine and sham marriage applicants alike, the criterion is a subjective analysis of two people's relationship and therefore difficult for an assessing officer to disprove. Spouse entry, therefore, has remained the category most open to abuse.

In order to arrange a sham marriage, however, the applicant needs a contact in Australia, a person willing to act as partner and sponsor or a go-between who can find such a partner. This possibly gives rise to the abuse of the visitor entry program and change of status provisions of the Australian immigration program. Over two million people a year enter as tourists or other visitors on visas for temporary stay in Australia. Once here they can apply to remain in Australia permanently if they meet certain legal criteria. They are also better placed to find marriage partners, whether for genuine or sham marriages.

Anecdotal evidence suggests that the change of status provision is subject to greater abuse than is the migrant entry program. In evidence to the JSCMR (1991, pp. 59–60), an Assistant Secretary of the Department of Immigration stated:

On the basis of departmental experience over a long period, I think most people involved in the department in this area would argue that people who apply via a sponsorship, an offshore application, are more likely to be genuine than people applying in Australia. Within the group applying in Australia, people applying on the basis of marriage are more likely to be genuine than people applying on the basis of a de facto relationship. This is the wisdom within the organisation, based on years of exposure to the case load.

Although figures on sham marriages are not available due to the difficulty of proving their fraudulent nature, the JSCMR (noting that investigation staff use 60 per cent of their time investigating on-shore marriage applications and requesting that a random selection of cases be analysed for better data) accepted that sham marriages were a significant problem. For this reason, in April 1991 the Immigration Minister announced new procedures for the granting of permanent resident status on spouse grounds. Henceforth an applicant would be given temporary status for two years, after which time permanent status would be granted only if the marriage was genuine and continuing, or, if the Australian partner had died, the marriage had been genuine and continuing and the applicant had created ties in Australia.

Mr Hand said the Government had decided on the tough new measures after considering reports from two bodies which had examined the issues —the National Population Council and the Joint Standing Committee (JSC) on Migration Regulations. (Media Release MPS 4/91)

Sham marriages have been exposed in several forms which the National Population Council, as reported by the JSCMR (1991, p. 61), referred to as Contractual Fraud and Unilateral Fraud:

Contractual fraud occurs where both parties conspire to marry or to assert a de facto relationship to enable a non-resident to seek and obtain permanent residence in Australia. The Australian partner typically would receive payment as consideration but other motives include sympathy for the situation of the non-resident, 'favours' to friends, relatives or community members, or philosophical objections to the restrictive immigration policy. In turn such contractual fraud may be arranged by the participants themselves or could be organised by an agency or a third party, usually for a fee.

One-sided marriage fraud, unilateral fraud, involves fraud on the part of the non-resident spouse who marries an unsuspecting Australian partner solely for the purpose of gaining permanent residence in Australia. The Australian partner, on the other hand, has entered into the relationship genuinely, frequently only to find him or herself abandoned once the desired resident status is achieved.

It is believed by immigration officers working in this field that contractual fraud is more common than unilateral fraud and that men enter into contractual fraud arrangements more often than women. This is, however, only supposition. Contractual fraud is more likely to come to the attention of investigators because several people are involved in, and aware of, the fraud before it is perpetrated. In the case of unilateral fraud, it may only come to light after the applicant has obtained permanent residence and deserted his or her unsuspecting partner. Several cases of unilateral fraud have come to the attention of the Family Court when one or other of the parties has applied for the court to find the marriage void.

Section 23(1)(d)(i) of the *Marriage Act 1961* states that a marriage is void if the consent of either party was not a 'real' consent because it was obtained by duress or fraud. Section 51 of the *Family Law Act 1975* provides for such a marriage to be annulled. In a discussion of such cases, Davis (1988, p. 154), in his article 'Fraud and Annulment of Marriage', reports the case of Deniz and Deniz, where a male had misled an Australian female into marriage in order to obtain permanent residence in Australia:

> Frederico J found as a fact that the respondent never had 'the slightest intention of fulfilling in any respect the obligations of marriage'. He had simply 'used the unfortunate applicant as a tool of his own convenience . . . He clearly deceived the applicant into marriage for his own personal ends, and with the intention of summarily rejecting her immediately after the ceremony'. Frederico J held that the respondent's conduct constituted fraud within the meaning of the Marriage Act . . . and granted a decree of nullity under the Family Law Act . . .

Davis also reports another sham marriage for immigration purposes in which the perpetrator of the sham was a woman and the applicant to the courts an Australian man. In that case the judge had found that the marriage was not void and that the case cited above had been wrongly decided, stating (p. 154):

> even if I am wrong, then in my view the facts themselves can be distinguished from those in the [other] case . . . The respondent in this case intended to stay with the petitioner for a sufficient length of time so that the immigration authorities would not say that the marriage had been one of convenience and entered into solely to enable her to remain in this country . . . In these circumstances it is not possible for us to say that, as in the case of Deniz, the respondent had not the slightest intention of fulfilling in any respect the obligations of marriage.

Disadvantage occurs to both men and women in sham-marriage situations in which the illegal activities are detected. As the previous section indicated, in discussing the vulnerability of Filipino women finding themselves in violent relationships once in Australia, people whose sham-marriage relationship breaks down are vulnerable to official sanctions. Women in such abusive relationships would presumably be in even greater danger than those in officially sanctioned marriages to Australian citizens, staying in a dangerous relationship longer because of the fear of the illegality of their situation being discovered. Are there, however, grounds for any claim that immigrant women as a whole (apart from those from particular countries) are at greater risk from their involvement in sham marriages than are immigrant men? There are no data comparing the involvement of men and women in scams and the nature of their circumstances there. Anecdotal evidence, in the form of the 'wisdom' of immigration officers working to apprehend offenders, suggests that men are more frequently involved in contractual fraud arrangements than are women. This does not reveal, however, whether immigrant women are commonly victimised in such schemes. Detailed examination of particular schemes might hint at gender bias in their operations, but probably never allow broad generalisations such as might be made if regional contexts (like that of the Filipinos), were explored. Where sham marriages persist for a while and break down, however, one might expect immigrant women participants to be worse off than immigrant men participants, for all the usual settlement reasons like difficulties in labour market mobility, as well as the threats of domestic violence. The fact that marriage-related criteria for immigration entry are the most readily exploited, however, suggests to us the need for critical appraisal of Australia's reliance for immigrants on marital status.

Thus, the concept of 'genuine and ongoing' marriages itself raises the notion of sham marriages, that is, marriages deliberately contrived for the purpose of gaining entry to Australia as immigrants. This practice, often organised for commercial gain, is based on a distortion of the concept of a genuine, continuing and even legal relationship. In the Annual Report of the Department of Immigration for 1990–1991 (DILGEA 1991h, p. 85, for example), contrived marriage rackets were listed as a national priority for investigation. The Report noted:

> By far the majority of the cases (twenty-five) were contrived marriage offences; at the end of 1990–91, four persons, two of whom are organisers, were awaiting trial on conspiracy charges relating to such marriages. Another seventy-five cases, sixty-five of which are for contrived marriages, were awaiting prosecution. The backlog of investigations awaiting completion remains unacceptably high. Four hundred and eighty cases have been identified for investigation. Of these, 260 are suspected contrived marriage cases.

Conclusion

In all these various marriage scenarios and the diverse relationships listed between marriage and immigration, how are women immigrants affected, keeping in mind that it is impossible to generalise about the significance of marital status for all women immigrants, or even identifiable groups of them? That is, what are the implications of the marriage–immigration tie for women? We focus our comments here on skills recognition, vulnerability in change of status and sham-marriage situations, and costs and benefits.

Women who migrate with their Principal Applicant husbands in the Independent and Concessional categories may be less advantaged than their husbands on arrival in Australia, because few would have been subjected to the points test and qualifications assessment. Therefore, their qualifications and skills would not have been assessed prior to their arrival, and would have to be assessed in Australia for entry to the appropriate labour market. The following is the general sequence of steps for having an immigrant's qualifications recognised, carried out overseas for Principal Applicants.

To decide how many points to allocate on the basis of skill, the assessor first determines the applicant's 'usual occupation' and then compares this information with the Australian Standard Classification of Occupations (ASCO) dictionary, which not only attempts to describe every job in Australia but also lists the qualifications and training needed to perform those jobs. The next task is to look at the applicant's education and formal qualifications to determine what their equivalent is in Australian terms. Many occupations, particularly the trades and professions, require specific training and are regulated by various boards and institutions. The electrical trades, for example, are regulated by the *Tradesman's Rights Regulations Act 1958* (No. 53), which is administered by the Department of Industrial Relations. To determine whether the applicant is qualified in one of these trades, the assessing officer sends the applicant's details to a Trades Assessor, for comment. This could be a lengthy process. Similarly, other trades and professions must be assessed by the National Office of Overseas Skills Recognition (NOOSR) of the Department of Employment, Education and Training (DEET), or a professional body or institute. All can take a considerable period of time.

The advantage to the Principal Applicant who enters under the Independent or Concessional categories is that his or her qualifications have already been partially or wholly assessed before entering Australia. The applicant therefore knows before embarking what the chances are of working in Australia in his or her occupation. Also, the already-assessed person may have papers in hand to start job hunting the day after arriving in Australia. Most such advantaged applicants would be male, for the simple reason that those occupations requiring such a process are often the same ones that, because of the need for formal qualifications, attract most points in the immigration points test. Occupations requiring formal qualifications are mostly located in male-dominated industries in Australia.

Once an applicant is found to meet the points test, the assessing officer need look no further and so the spouse's qualifications would not be assessed. Accompanying spouses, therefore, do not as often have the same advantage as Principal Applicant spouses. As couples commonly put the male first, the female will less often have her qualifications considered and therefore will not have the advantage of being given any guidance on how she will fare in the Australian work force, let alone being given documents saying her qualifications are recognised. For this she has to wait until she arrives in Australia, only then putting in train the lengthy process described.

The same lack of advantage holds true for any person entering under any other than the points-tested categories as Principal Applicant and who works in an occupation which needs formal qualifications in Australia. For example, the nurse immigrating to Australia as a spouse could not know whether he or she will be able to work in that profession until after arriving in Australia. As more women than men enter in the Preferential Family category and as 'accompanying' spouses in the Skill categories, more women might be expected to face this problem.

Women are much more vulnerable, and more likely than men to experience difficulties while awaiting the result of change of status applications. For anyone temporarily in Australia applying for permanent residence, the time frame for consideration of their application has generally been anything from six months to a year. Those applying on the basis of a marriage or de facto marital relationship with an Australian citizen or resident, are faced with maintaining that relationship until the application is decided. Having an uncertain status leaves many vulnerable to violent partners, as has been explained already (Mottee 1992).

Though evidence is not available to support a strong claim that women are more vulnerable, also, in sham-marriage situations, we consider it possible that in contractual fraud arrangements in which men predominate, men may make use of sympathetic female friends. (Though they may also have access to the resources needed, like large sums of money and access to a network of organisers.) In the case of unilateral fraud, as there is no evidence as to the frequency of such cases nor the gender of the applicants, we consider it likely that women make 'better' targets than men for offers of an apparently genuine marriage.

Finally, the greater numbers of women immigrating as part of relationships with Principal Applicant men, suggest that women may bear disproportionately the inevitable social, economic, physical and emotional disruption of the immigration process. That is, the number of women immigrating to be with their husbands in Australia raises the question of how many are giving up their own familial, social and occupation networks, their culture and language, in the interests of their male partner.

> One woman, who had not been to Australia prior to migrating . . . had done so at the suggestion of her prospective husband who was living in Australia and knew that finding a job in Malaysia would be difficult.

In all it appears that three women considered migrating because of others, usually because of husband's job prospects and for their children's future prospects. (Madden & Young 1993a)

If migrating means giving up certain benefits associated with one's place of origin such as the recognition of educational qualifications, knowledge of the language, family networks and familiarity with the job market, and taking up other benefits in the place of destination such as economic security and a more robust job market, then how much more disadvantaged are women who migrate for marriage than men? Tienda and Booth (1991) have commented, however, on the difficulties of drawing any generalisable conclusions on this matter.

Contrary to everyday views which may see personal and marriage relationships as a matter of chance and merely of individual preference, there are many structuring forces inside and external to Australia which create conditions favouring the development of relationships (including marriage) between men and women and which also stimulate population flows as a result of immigration. Marital status is a more important factor for women in immigration to Australia than it is for men. Furthermore, it can be more important for women than almost any other factor. It follows that undesirable results of marriage–immigration such as dislocation from the work force or tenuous legal status are likely to be borne, proportionately, by more women than men.

The consequences of marriage immigration, bearing as they do more heavily on women than men, raise specific issues to do with gender equity. Ironically, there is a difficulty here. If marital status were removed or de-emphasised as an immigration selection criterion, this could result in the exclusion of many women who would be unable to meet other criteria based on attributes such as language, age, educational level, qualifications and skills. Clearly, any reduction in emphasis on marital status as a selection criterion would have to be accompanied by a broadening of the still masculinist definitions of skill. This is a long-term project.

In the short term, to help ease the burden of the settlement process for many women, the Department of Immigration could, for example, adopt a process of facilitating qualifications assessment for any immigration applicant who appears to be eligible in any category and who intends to enter the work force in Australia. This applies in cases where the claimed occupation requires formal assessment of qualifications in order to work in the specified field. This could be done for all working age persons included in the application. It should reduce the lag times between arrival in Australia and entering the work force in the chosen field. As well, of course, a broader range of competencies than the 'skills' conventionally recognised and associated largely with male occupations and training, could be included in immigration selection criteria. These could be set out quite explicitly to reflect the things that women do.

Chapter 4: The state's influence on settlement prospects for immigrant women—the labour market and the 'double burden'

This chapter moves on to settlement issues, departing from the sole focus on immigrant entry and selection policy and procedures which have been the concern of chapters 2 and 3. The intent in this chapter is to contrast the circumstances of immigrant women as 'settlers', with the circumstances of other groups, especially immigrant men, but also Australia-born women. This will be done in order to demonstrate that the settlement of immigrants is a gendered process and, further, to indicate how the policies and practices of the state contribute to the gendering of settlement. One set of influences on the gendered nature of settlement is the immigrant selection practices of the Australian Government—it is proposed that it makes a difference which category immigrant men and women enter Australia under, in ways some of which have been mentioned already. There are also, however, other government policies specifically to do with settlement that treat immigrant men and women differently.

To the degree that women who have entered Australia as immigrants are disadvantaged relative to immigrant men in the settlement process, then claims can be made that gender equity does not prevail. Of course, as noted in chapter 1, there are many influences on the way people experience the settlement process, and not all are related to the activities of governments concerning immigrants. Some are government-related, however, and some of these are discussed in this chapter. (The chapter does not seek to compare the circumstances of immigrant women once in Australia with their situations prior to immigration: this is a complex gender equity issue, involving many comparative judgments about the social relations of origins and destinations. Authors who have broached it in assessing immigrant women's altered positions due to migrations of different sorts include Tienda and Booth 1991; Barsotti and Lecchini 1991; Elley 1985, 1988; Phizacklea 1983; Akcehk and Elley 1988.)

Participation in one important aspect of daily life—the paid labour force—has been selected as basic to the settlement process for immigrants. With this topic in mind, government influences on the participation of immigrant women in Australian society are examined and suggestions about the gender equity entailed are drawn out. It is not claimed that women and men should be the same in the way they participate in societal institutions and practices, but that the state (and indeed other bodies) should not influence men and women in such a way as to differentiate their participation markedly.

The basic gender equity claim to be advanced in this chapter is that immigrant women have been disadvantaged relative to immigrant men in the period since the Second World War because of the 'double burden' of work they have had little choice in assuming. A high proportion of immigrant women have worked full time in the paid labour force for some decades now, years before a similar proportion of Australia-born women did so. This is an indirect, locational outcome of government immigration policy because immigrants went (and still go) to major metropolitan areas to live, at a time when work was available in those places. This incurred relatively high living costs for immigrant households and therefore a need for women to take on paid work (as well as the domestic labour which was already their lot).

The chapter begins with an overview of immigrant women's place in contemporary Australian labour markets, with some reference being made to comparison of this situation with that of the past few decades in Australia, and to overseas countries with similar immigration policies and practices. Then follows material on the locational reasons why this situation arose in Australia, producing the 'double burden' for those immigrant women working long hours in both paid and unpaid jobs.

Immigrant women in Australian labour markets

The recent broadening of conceptual thinking about the nature of the work that women and men do has caused some authors to argue that women's relationship to work is different and concepts drawn from the analysis of immigrant men in paid work do not necessarily apply to immigrant women in paid work. This reflects a possibly emerging view that gender is a greater differentiator of status and power in the labour market than ethnicity (see Boyd, Mulvihill & Myles 1991 and Woo 1985, whose discussions might be interpreted in this way). Different labour markets are created for 'migrant and racial-ethnic women', argues Glenn (1986, p. 15), because of societal stratification on gender and racial–ethnic lines. Further, the reproductive tasks undertaken by women, of 'sustaining family life and transmitting cultural values' are even more arduous for immigrant women than for other women, and so cement immigrant women into certain labour market segments the more effectively.

With the usual qualifications about the usefulness of labour force statistics, for example about the levels of disaggregation they permit and the fact that domestic labour is not part of the 'work' they measure, the evidence on aspects of immigrant women's working lives in Australia will now be considered, and then ways in which the state has influenced the outcomes described.

Labour force participation

When considering people's labour market participation, comparison is usually made between overseas-born and Australia-born women and men—a four-way comparison. However, it is often also the case that different groups of women are compared with each other, to assess their relative performance in what is a very gender-segregated labour market. Many of the official data presented below do this, allowing a comparison of immigrant women most commonly with Australia-born women, rather than with immigrant men, as has generally been the tendency in this paper.

In Australia by the late 1980s, rates of participation by immigrant women in the paid labour force had been overtaken by the rates of participation by Australia-born women.[2] In November 1992, the labour force participation rate for women in Australia was 51.3 per cent; with the rates for Australia-born and overseas-born women being 54.1 and 48.0 per cent respectively. Among those born overseas, however, women born in main English-speaking countries had a labour force participation rate of 54.4 per cent, compared with 43.7 per cent for those born in other countries. This is in contrast to the majority of the post-Second World War period, when participation rates for NESB women were generally higher than those of their Australia-born counterparts. However, these figures mask some of the more disaggregated trends in the data, including:

☐ labour force participation rates over the 1980s increased most for married Australia-born females; married immigrant women were already well represented in the paid work force, so their participation rates have not increased markedly;

☐ unmarried immigrant women are less likely to be employed than married ones; the reverse is true of the Australia-born;

☐ growth of the participation of married Australia-born women is most likely to be in part-time work, reflecting the jobs available in the 1980s;

☐ overseas-born and in particular NESB women in the paid labour force are more likely to work longer hours. Recent data indicate that more Australia-born women work 1–19 hours per week and more overseas-born women work 41 hours or over each week (ABS 1991b, p. 84). Of those women not in the labour force who expressed a wish to join it, more Australia-born and English-speaking-background immigrant women wanted part-time work, and more NESB immigrant women wanted full-time work. (ABS 1991b, p. 30)

A report of the Commonwealth State Council on NESB Women's Issues (Alcorso & Harrison 1991) makes useful points about labour force participation figures like these, that are used to contrast the working circumstances of immigrant and Australia-born women. They emphasise that rather than concentrating on the labour *supply* data, that is the characteristics of the women themselves, in describing the range of employment circumstances between the 'groups' of women, attempts should also be made to consider the labour *market* (or demand) situations making jobs available to these different groups. For example, at a time when Australia-born women began to enter the labour force in increasing numbers, part-time jobs were on offer and part-time jobs are what they largely took up (which caused which is hard to unravel). When Southern European women arrived in the three decades after the Second World War, manufacturing jobs, usually full time, were available and possible for people without English language competence. A focus on the labour market in particular places is necessary to understand the employment options available to immigrant women at particular times. What is the evidence, then, about the industries and occupations in which immigrant women work, compared with those of immigrant men and the Australia-born?

Occupational and industrial allocation

It has long been commented that immigrant women in Australia occupy 'the worst jobs' in manufacturing industry, in factories or in outwork. Bottomley (1984) has made a 'list of difficulties' of Mediterranean women in Australia, including those of their workplaces, and Rush and Steen (1987) have presented information about the working lives of Spanish-speaking women. The Centre for Urban Research and Action (CURA) (Storer 1976) report, which examined the circumstances of 710 immigrant women working in thirty factories in Melbourne, is generally recognised as the first major study to have documented the dreadful working conditions of immigrant women in manufacturing industry in Australia.

The labour market segments 'ladder' identified by authors like Collins (1988), in which NESB immigrant women occupy the lowest rung, has become an accepted part of many statements about immigrants' labour force status. Immigrant women have clearly felt the results of the fact that Australia is the most occupationally sex-segregated country in the Organisation for Economic Co-operation and Development (OECD).

As to industrial distribution, NESB women are heavily concentrated in manufacturing industry. Between 1971 and 1990, manufacturing industry employed, proportionately, twice as many overseas-born women as Australia-born (Webber, Campbell & Fincher 1990, p. 7). This was still the case in November 1992, when women born in non-English-speaking countries made up over 25 per cent of female workers in the manufacturing industry (as compared with 12.1 per cent of all employed women). Over 20 per cent of employed NESB women worked in manufacturing industry (compared with 8.4 per cent of Australia-born women). In contrast, the distribution across industries of employed female immigrants from English-speaking backgrounds (ESBs) was similar to that of Australia-born women. Female immigrants from ESBs were overrepresented in community services, finance, property and business services. Overseas-born women (and in particular Italians, Chinese, Polish, USSR, Cypriots, Lebanese, Turkish and Vietnamese) were, at the end of the 1980s, about 1.3 times as segregated within manufacturing industry as the Australia-born. Further:

Despite slow declines in the levels of industrial segregation over time, the relative position of the four gender [male and female] and birthplace groups has not altered: some 25% of overseas born females, 20% of Australian born females, 12% of overseas born males and 8% of Australian born males would have to change their industry in order to match the industrial structure of the total employed population in Australia. (Webber, Campbell & Fincher 1990, p. 8)

Many females are also employed in the wholesale and retail industry. At November 1992, this industry accounted for 23.1 per cent of employed Australia-born females, with the corresponding figures for women from ESBs and NESBs being 18.5 and 17.7 per cent respectively. NESB workers in this industry probably make up a good proportion of the self-employed.

Alcorso (1991, pp. 42 ff.) has shown that newly arriving immigrant women from non-English-speaking countries continue to enter manufacturing employment faster than longer-term residents. However, her data reveal, from censuses between 1971 and 1986, that manufacturing industry was providing fewer jobs for newly arrived immigrant women by the mid-1980s. This is consistent with the decline in the growth of manufacturing in Australia over this time. The various birthplace groups, however, have had different experiences with manufacturing employment. In 1981, for example, over 65 per cent of Vietnamese and Turkish women who had arrived in the previous five years were in manufacturing work, whereas 40–45 per cent was the equivalent figure for the Lebanese and Latin Americans (Lebanese women were 66.7 per cent in manufacturing employment in 1971) (Alcorso 1991, p. 43). It is interesting to note that American evidence of immigrant women's industrial allocation during settlement has similar suggestions of their disproportionate presence in manufacturing and in declining sectors (Tienda, Jensen & Bach 1984).

Regarding the occupations of immigrant women, ABS (1991b, p. 72) summarises the situation in Australia at the end of 1990 as follows:

> females born in English-speaking countries had a similar occupational distribution to the Australian-born. ... By comparison, females born overseas in non-English-speaking countries were relatively under-represented in professional (10.5 per cent), clerical (25.2 per cent) and sales and personal service occupations (16.4 per cent). On the other hand they were over-represented in the labouring and related occupations (24.2 per cent), and as plant and machine operators and drivers (8.4 per cent). Within the major occupation group 'labourers and related workers', 35,400 females born in non-English-speaking countries were employed as trades assistants and factory hands and 27 800 were employed as cleaners. Data from the 1986 Census showed a concentration of Vietnamese-born females (51.5 per cent), southern-European-born females (30.3 per cent), and western Asian or Middle Eastern females (20.0 per cent) employed as factory hands, cleaners, and plant and machine operators and drivers relative to the Australian-born (8.0 per cent).

Canadian data show the same patterns of occupational distribution (Boyd 1986, p. 56).

In the United States the concentration of particular birthplace groups in low-status occupations raises policy concerns to do with the possibilities of discrimination against these groups (Tienda, Jensen & Bach 1984). It has also been claimed in overseas studies of Canada, the United States and Israel, that immigrant women have never attained occupational status similar to that of native-born women (Hartman & Hartman 1983). On this, see also Boyd (1987) for Canada, Grossman (1984) for Sweden and Lie (1983) for Norway.

This raises the issue of occupational attainment and mobility— even if immigrant women start out in low-status jobs, do they, as soon as they settle, improve their positions in the labour market? ABS (1991b, pp. 73-4) describes the occupational distribution of women relative to their educational qualifications, from the 1986 Census. This is an indication of occupational attainment. It shows that:

❑ of women with a tertiary qualification, the overseas-born, especially those of NESB, were underrepresented as professionals and overrepresented as paraprofessionals; those of NESB with tertiary qualifications were more likely to be clerks, labourers and related workers than the Australia-born with similar qualifications;

❑ of women with non-tertiary post-school qualifications, the occupational distributions differed less, and the major variation was that immigrant women of NESB were more likely to find work as labourers and related workers or plant and machine operators and less likely to be employed as paraprofessionals;

❏ of women without post-school qualifications, immigrants of NESB were less likely than the Australia-born women to be clerks, salespersons and personal services workers, and more likely to be plant and machine operators and labourers and related workers.

For NESB immigrant women, then, whether they have post-school or university qualifications appears to make less difference to their employment prospects than it does to those of Australia-born women.

The significant question to be asked after seeing such data is whether this situation improves for immigrant women in Australia with period of residence. Those who attribute lack of occupational attainment by immigrant women to their lack of English language competence, for example, would expect to be able to demonstrate that with period of residence and (therefore, one assumes) improvement in English language skills, immigrant women would experience significant upward mobility in their employment circumstances. Indeed, for those women born in NES countries but speaking English only, or who speak English very well, there is likely to be achievement of an occupational distribution similar to the Australia-born or those born in English-speaking countries (ABS 1991b, p. 77). For NESB immigrant women in general, however, unlike the situation for immigrants as a whole, upward occupational mobility has not been found to occur. ABS (1991b, pp. 71–2) cites a number of studies that have found from statistical analysis little evidence of occupational mobility as period of residence grows.

As the ABS study notes, however, census data 'cannot provide information about occupational mobility or advancement among overseas-born females' (1991b, p. 75)—censuses provide cross-sectional data not longitudinal data. This implies that other studies that have collected data about changes in individuals' lives over time will be better able to answer questions about occupational mobility. (Although, if these are studies based on lengthy interviews, they will obviously have the disadvantage of a more limited sample size than the Census.) Such studies tend to focus on particular birthplace groups, or industries, or both in certain locations—this is clearly because of the limits to interview studies of the sort that can identify occupational mobility and perhaps its meaning for individuals. What is the evidence from such work?

One recent survey of 272 Greece-, Yugoslavia- and Viet Nam-born workers in Melbourne used recall data from the immigrants to gain descriptions of the sequence of their paid employment, from before arrival in Australia to the present (Campbell, Fincher & Webber 1991). The year of arrival of the immigrants ranged from 1952 to 1987. For a very high proportion of both men and women in the sample, the initial job found in Australia was a lower-skilled job in manufacturing industry, regardless of qualifications or work experience from the country of origin. What happened after this, particularly for women? For this sample, the study concludes that:

> there is apparent upward occupational mobility for 15 of the 93 women whose first job in manufacturing was as an operator or labourer. Similarly, there is apparent upward occupational mobility for 24 of the 155 males whose first job in manufacturing was as an operator or labourer. (Campbell, Fincher & Webber 1991, p. 184)

Nonetheless, attention must be paid to two things: first, that the largest group of men and women in the sample are those who left the labour force after a period in a 'low skilled' manufacturing job, and this is what accounts for the decline in significance of operating and labouring occupations among sample members; and second, for those who moved into self-employment or small business, there needs to be examination of what this actually means (for example, is it a mis-classification of outwork, which is more properly 'disguised waged work' than 'self-employment') before upward occupational mobility can be claimed. The authors' summary of the evidence on job 'paths' is that, overall, people remain in similar jobs in manufacturing industry to those they entered (Campbell, Fincher & Webber 1991, p. 188).

Alcorso's (1991) study of over 100 immigrant women living and working in Sydney produced remarkably similar findings. Despite these women's varied pre-immigration experiences and qualifications, they ended up in:

> similarly low status, unpleasant and unrewarding jobs—jobs which for many represented substantial downward mobility. These women experienced the segmentation of the labour market as a constraining framework, directing them towards certain types of jobs and limiting their opportunities to move out of them. (Alcorso 1991, p. 8)

The study revealed much movement of women between jobs of similar status, especially for new arrivals but also for those resident longer in Australia. There was far less movement to higher-status occupations (Alcorso 1991, p. 68). Other Australian studies have hinted at similar conclusions (Manderson & Inglis 1984; Rush & Steen 1987).

Unemployment and underemployment

Unemployment and underemployment are the final issues in this glance at immigrant women's labour force characteristics. Between 1985 and 1992, unemployment rates for immigrant women were higher than those for their Australia-born counterparts. These rates declined for both groups in the period to 1990, but fluctuated more for immigrant women than for those born in Australia. In fact, Alcorso and Harrison (1991, p. 12) state:

> NESB women have generally suffered more unemployment than any other group in Australian society except Aborigines and people with disabilities.

The unemployment rate for NESB women rose from a low point of 2.7 in 1973 to a peak of 12.5 during the 1982-3 recession, to 8.0 per cent in May, 1989.

In November 1992 the unemployment rate for women from NESB countries was 15.1 per cent, while the corresponding rates for ESB and Australian-born women were 7.4 and 8.5 per cent respectively. Among immigrant women, those from Asia had the highest unemployment rates. Unemployment rates were higher throughout the 1980s for recently arrived immigrants than for those who had been in Australia for longer periods. This was particularly so for NESB women. The ABS (1991b) has also found that immigrant women in 1990 who had come to Australia as Principal Applicants since 1970, had lower rates of unemployment than those who had entered Australia as the partners of Principal Applicants over the same period (1991b, p. 34).

Alcorso and Harrison (1991) make specific comments about immigrant women and unemployment in the 1990-93 recession. They find:

❏ that though women are recorded as experiencing lower rates of unemployment than men in the current recession, this is not the case for NESB immigrant women whose unemployment rates are also much higher than those of ESB immigrant women and the Australia-born;

❏ while the average duration of women's unemployment has grown in the recession to nine months (as of August 1991), that of NESB women is even longer—about eleven months; and

❏ fewer unemployed NESB immigrant women than those Australia-born or from an ESB have worked full time in the last two years (Alcorso & Harrison 1991, pp. 19-20).

Data on underemployment show that overseas-born women have consistently had lower underemployment rates than women born in Australia. This has been so for the last three ABS surveys on this topic—1985, 1988 and 1991. ABS researchers (1991b, pp. 45-6) claim that this is not surprising, because fewer overseas-born than Australia-born women work part time with the desire to enter full-time work (they work full time already, full-time jobs being characteristic of the industries in which they are often located). The study also shows (pp. 46-7) that immigrant women take up unemployment benefits at a slower rate than Australia-born women. However, hidden unemployment may be disproportionately represented among immigrant women—those who are hidden unemployed, or discouraged workers, are not recorded as seeking work.

How have the policies and practices of the Australian state given rise to these employment patterns of immigrant women, in particular to the sustained presence of NESB women immigrants in lower-status occupations?

First, have immigration selection policies, detailed in chapter 2, influenced these labour market outcomes? It is clear that in those countries in which women immigrants are selected precisely for employment in 'women's work' like domestic service, then women of certain birthplace groups will have very high labour force participation rates because they are involved in such schemes. Canada is one such country (see Boyd & Taylor 1986). Australia, however, does *not* seek women actively for such work in its contemporary policy. We have suggested in earlier chapters that the administrative mechanisms of designating one immigrant applicant in a household the Principal Applicant tends to disadvantage women because it is less often they who are so designated. The disadvantage of this consists in the fact that the woman's skills and qualifications will not be assessed until after her arrival in Australia, causing her, possibly, a long wait before employment commensurate with her skills may be sought. It is possible that a need for money could force a non-Principal Applicant in this situation to accept a less suitable position, and remain there. We have also indicated that women rely disproportionately on immigration criteria that construct them as dependants of men when they immigrate to Australia. Unlike some other countries, however, Australia does not deny language and other settlement services to the dependants of its new immigrants (see Fincher, Foster, Giles and Preston (1993) for a comparison of Australia with Canada in this respect).

The effect of Australian immigrant selection on the subsequent employment situations of immigrants, then is, in our view, best understood as an indirect effect. It is a *locational* effect—that is, Australian immigrant selection drew to Australia in the post-Second World War decades large numbers of immigrants who settled in the particular places where manufacturing was offering them jobs. The jobs were primarily in major cities where housing costs were high. Women in immigrant households found themselves needing to work to gain income to support themselves in these expensive urban locations. Accordingly, Manderson and Inglis (1984) have noted that women (here, Turkish) became involved in paid work as well as domestic labour once in Australia, whereas often they had neither done this before, nor intended it after immigration.

The effect of Australian immigrant selection on the settlement process, then, was a product of its context. Immigrants were chosen in the early post-Second World War decades to work in expanding industrial plants. This they did, and thereby incurred the costs of a life in major metropolitan areas. From that time, despite the decline in opportunities within manufacturing industries, immigrants have continued to locate in the places (the major cities) where those from their countries of origin have gone before. Again, immigrant households find themselves primarily in major metropolitan areas where housing costs are high, and where more than one adult income is often needed to support a family.

This indirect locational effect of immigration selection has also had gendered outcomes, in the form of the 'double burden' of work that immigrant women have assumed. The labour force participation rates for immigrant women of NESB describe their persistently high employment levels, and the fact that for years their jobs have been full-time, and often in manufacturing (like their husbands). What the data cannot indicate is the nature of the domestic responsibilities they have carried as well.

Bittman's analysis of the 1987 Australian time-use survey, however, provides a statistical starting point in contemplating the double burden of present-day immigrant women. He remarks (1991, p. 57) that NESB immigrants in Australia are now clearly divided along 'male breadwinner and female homemaker' lines, though this may in part reflect the high levels of unemployment of NESB women. NESB women also spend the least time of all groups in leisure pursuits. According to Bittman, they spend the smallest amount of time in paid work (officially recorded), and the greatest in unpaid work. In particular, these women spend much time caring for other people's children, and more time than those in similar age-groups in the Australia-born population in child-care tasks generally (Bittman 1991, p. 56). These findings with regard to NESB immigrant women are against a general background of information that the time men spend doing unpaid work does not increase as their wives spend more time in paid employment. Furthermore:

> the statistically most powerful predictor of paid and unpaid work time of women was marriage. Marriage is three times more influential than the next most important factor which is the number of paid hours worked in the previous week. (Bittman 1991, p. 3)

Qualitative reports provide further information on immigrant women's post-immigration workload. A study by Kunek (1988) focused on women immigrants of Greek origin and was based on their self-reporting at a seminar in Melbourne. The women's oral testimony referred to family life in Greece and Cyprus and in Australia. It provided a familiar picture of immigrants coming from a patriarchal tradition in which there was strong gender role differentiation in the family and a relatively low participation in paid work. They immigrated to a country where, to achieve satisfactory settlement, many of the women were forced to undertake paid work but the requirements of language and education level precluded most of them from obtaining anything other than factory work. This led to the 'double burden' and often an acceptance by mothers that they must sacrifice themselves for husband and children. Much the same trends were noted by Vasta (1985) in her study of long-settled Italo-Australian women in Brisbane. McCallum and Gelfand's (1990) study of daughters caring for older immigrants in Australia confirms the greater burden assumed by these women, even where they did not go out to paid work.

Political involvement

If this double burden has been carried by NESB (in particular) immigrant women for many years, as the statistical and qualitative data indicate, then it is no wonder that in another major 'public sphere' of Australian activity, politics and political activism of various sorts, these same immigrant women have not been very visible. They simply have not had time. Political participation in such circumstances would be a question of resources, English language competence and life stage, with those women not needing to work in the paid labour force for long hours and in 'unskilled' jobs, and those women without dependants, being more likely to be politically active. (One must emphasise, however, that all formal political institutions in Australia are heavily biased in favour of male participation.) Even in unionised workplaces, where NESB workers, and women, have made up significant percentages of union membership (ACTU 1991; Victorian Trades Hall Council 1991), immigrant women and men are greatly underrepresented in senior positions of the trade union movement (Miltenyi 1988, p. 35; Nicolaou 1991, p. 191; Bertone & Griffin 1992).

And indeed, when immigrant women who are active politically have been profiled, they are generally found in ethnic community organisations, these being effective politically, accessible, and a social network as well (WEN 1990; Pohjola 1991; Seitz & Kilmartin 1987). Furthermore, in a pilot study interviewing 102 women from six ethnic groups in Melbourne, major barriers to broader political participation were found to be: lack of confidence, lack of education (including English language competence), advanced age, little time and information (especially about advisory bodies) and cultural expectations of family role. Overseas-born women were more likely to be involved in community organisations or to represent community organisations on advisory bodies, whereas women of immigrant background but who were born in Australia were more likely to be involved at the State or national level. Joiners have these characteristics: they are usually under 35 years of age, have no family responsibilities, are higher income earners, and are less likely to need interpreters (Seitz & Kilmartin 1987).

Our own brief survey, conducted in 1991, inquired of nine women about the nature of the political participation in which they and other NESB women engaged. Each of the nine had participated at a senior level in ethnic community organisations.[3]

Between them, they had been members or office bearers, on a voluntary basis, of over twenty ethnic-based organisations. These included women's organisations, ethnic community organisations, umbrella organisations for many ethnic communities and ethnic organisations or programs formulated and funded by government bodies or departments. The sorts of issues they have pursued relating to NESB women have ranged from information on rights and representation within the political and legal system, through health, welfare and education, to social and cultural activities.

The women were asked to characterise NESB women who participate in ethnic organisations, that is, who are politically active over and above participation in Australia's compulsory voting system. Though their comments were diverse, they make clear the class and life-stage characteristics of political organisers and participants that we have noted. Some comments were:

> They have to be fairly competent in English. Either they are children of migrants or they're educated migrants. They are women with an education who have a career in that field and who can be outspoken because they are working in the area and they are able to articulate the issues.

> Those who are more involved are those who have been here a number of years, who are more settled . . . they feel ready to help people.

> They are usually busy women, in other words they actually run a family, hold down a job as well as be involved in the organisation. They are very articulate. Most of them are professional women.

> We are more in the elite group than in the grass roots, those of us in the organising level. Most of those who are in a position to organise or to convene these types of activities are usually the same people because there are very few of us who are able to do that.

> There is a group of women who are essentially first generation but happen to be blessed with parents who gave them a lot of opportunity and who were socialised to talk and to have a point of view. The core group are articulate both in English and in their mother tongue.

The next two sections of the chapter deal with the issue of the locations of immigrants arriving in Australia in the last forty-five years. First, where have immigrants settled, and what have been the processes leading them there? This discussion substantiates the claim that the double burden assumed by immigrant women on arrival in Australia was in part due to the costs of living in the places they went. The high costs of living there caused immigrant women's entry into the paid labour force. The gender equity issue in this situation arises from the fact that the women continued their full load of domestic responsibilities at the same time as they took on full-time paid work. There is no evidence that immigrant men did the same.

Secondly, the spatial incidence of two settlement 'services' important for women—child care and English language services—will be briefly discussed. The point to note here is that the opportunity to use these services occurs most readily in metropolitan rather than rural areas, thus reinforcing the reasons for immigrants to settle in metropolitan places.

93

Where immigrants settle

The locations in which immigrants to Australia settle have been summarised in reports such as Wooden et al. (1990), Borowski and Shu
(1992), Fincher (1991) and Dawkins et al. (1991). None of these
reports indicates whether the settlement patterns of male and female
immigrants are similar—there is no reason to think they would not
be, although the reasons why male and female immigrants (often
within family units) choose the locations they do and the consequences of those choices may differ. There is limited information,
however, on the different rationales for locational choices made by
economic, family and refugee class immigrants.

The major points to note about the locations selected by immigrants now, and in the past few decades, are the following:

1. Most immigrants, four out of every five in fact, settle in Australia's
   five largest cities—Sydney, Melbourne, Brisbane, Perth and
   Adelaide. Immigration being associated with increased urban-
   isation of the population is something that occurs in Canada also,
   where most immigrants locate in Toronto (especially), Vancouver
   and Montreal. In the United States, certain major cities receive
   disproportionate numbers of certain immigrant groups (Webber
   1991, p. 28). Sydney and Melbourne are the most popular destinations among the Australian cities. Sydney presently receives
   about one-third of all immigrants (though it also loses many
   people through outmigration from the city) (National Population
   Council, Population Issues Committee 1992, p. 8). All this means
   that immigrants are overrepresented in Australia's large cities; in
   the 1980s, for example, while Sydney held 22 per cent of the
   Australian population, it received 36 per cent of net overseas
   immigrants (Borowski & Shu 1992, p. 81).

2. Particular policy groupings of immigrants (economic, family and
   humanitarian) and particular birthplace groups are now tending to
   locate in some cities rather than others, though all are overrepresented in Sydney. Borowski and Shu (1992, p. 81) try to make a
   clear-cut link between the characteristics of immigrants and their
   recent settlement patterns, arguing that family immigrants go to
   where their sponsors are, and economic immigrants follow
   employment opportunities.

3. The distribution within Australian States of immigrants of different birthplaces is summarised and thoroughly referenced by Hugo
   (1990, pp. 78ff.). There is, as he describes, a plethora of studies
   investigating the extent to which immigrant groups are spatially
   concentrated within States and within metropolitan areas. Hugo's
   summary is an expert one and we do not need to repeat it. It
   establishes that those immigrants with the fewest language and
   cultural differences from Anglo-Australians are the least concen-

trated or segregated; this includes immigrants born in the United Kingdom, the Republic of Ireland and countries of Europe (especially of Eastern Europe, and the Netherlands, Poland and Germany). Immigrants whose settlement patterns exhibit the greatest residential concentrations are those born in the former Yugoslavia, Malta, Greece, Italy, the Middle East and (in particular) Viet Nam (Hugo 1990, pp. 79–81).

This general pattern of segregation and dispersal of different birthplace groups seems to have been the case in Australian cities since the early 1960s. Burnley (1985, and see Burnley 1974), however, has added considerable detail by identifying the types of urban settings in which certain birthplace groups settled at different times. He traces, for example, the concentrated settlement of Italians, Greeks and Maltese in central and inner Sydney and Melbourne in the 1960s, and the dispersal of the British and displaced persons in a range of more outlying suburbs and in public housing estates. In the 1970s, Burnley (1985, p. 192) notes among immigrants a 'regrouping process . . . as families, once in the owner-buyer market, wished to provide ample space for their children, and as wider kinship groups wished to regroup in relatively close proximity to each other'. The old concentrations of particular birthplace groups were often then bypassed by new arrivals moving directly to suburbs further out. Later immigrant streams, in particular the Indochinese, located in Sydney's south-west and central western suburbs rather than in the inner city, because in these suburbs were found the migrant hostels in which new arrivals (particularly refugees) originally stayed and because these suburbs by the 1980s were the sites of cheaper rental accommodation (Burnley 1985, p. 194, and see Horvath & Engels 1985). In the literature that establishes the spatial locations of immigrant settlement in Australia, mention of women and men is largely confined to discussion of their educational and occupational attributes. When settlement locations and movements are noted, it is invariably 'immigrants' as gender-undifferentiated groups that are considered. They are family units, birthplace-based communities, or occupational groupings, not men and women.

What are the reasons identified in the literature for immigrants' urban settlement preferences? To analyse the gender (and other) relations that give rise to the broad locational choices commonly made by immigrants, of where they will live, it would be useful to have information on how the decisions to migrate are made among members of households or family groups. As Hugo (1990, p. 30) indicates, however, little research attention has been paid to this in Australia.

Statistical analyses of contemporary data indicate that the 'size and age of the existing stock of immigrants from particular countries in particular states is very important in influencing the size of immigration inflows' (Dawkins et al., 1991, p. xiii). This applies to all categories of immigrant in the study from which it comes, which centred on flows of immigrants to South Australia, Tasmania and Western Australia (not States receiving the largest numbers of immigrant settlers). This finding was attributed to immigrants' choosing to locate in destinations in which friends, relatives or other contacts lived, especially since these places were therefore the ones about which the immigrants had most information. As well, economic immigrants were particularly concerned about job opportunities; humanitarian immigrants particularly focused on housing and house prices (Dawkins et al., 1991, p. xiii). Links to the education system, through having previously been a student in Australia, were likely to generate subsequent immigration flows to a particular location; and proximity of a given country to a particular Australian State or city was felt likely to attract immigrants from that country to that State. Note, however, that these interpretations of locational choices in the Dawkins et al. report are not based on a large survey of immigrants themselves, but rather on quantitative databases and on the views of 'key agents' like federal and State government officials and leaders of ethnic organisations. A recent Australian Council of Social Service report (ACOSS 1992) on the role of residential location and mobility in the settlement process confirms some of the above findings, stressing the importance for immigrants of living in locations that are 'familiar' in some way, like living near people from one's own ethnic group.

Generalisations about the reasons for and nature of immigrants' locational choices cannot be made in an historical vacuum: what people do and why has to be seen in the context of the opportunities available at certain places at particular times, and also the constraints likely to be present for immigrants at certain places and times (Hugo 1990, pp. 81ff.). Immigrants arriving in Australia in the 1950s and 1960s (and they were of particular birthplace groups, especially Southern European) took up employment opportunities in Melbourne, Sydney and Adelaide because manufacturing was then expanding in those places. Housing locations were chosen partly because of proximity to these jobs. As well (as has already been referred to), housing opportunities (especially cheap rental and purchase) in Australian cities at this time were mainly in inner areas. This is less the case now that gentrification has altered the cost of housing in inner areas, and much housing accessible to new immigrants is located in outer urban areas. During periods when government residential hostels were providing housing for many newly arrived immigrants, subsequent housing and employment choices were often made in the vicinity of this initial accommodation (Hugo 1990).

More recently, analysis of the process of chain migration permitted by Australian family reunion criteria for immigrant selection has demonstrated why it is that certain birthplace groups are now expanding, in places where their sponsoring families are located (Birrell 1990). Others have noted that it is not just newly arriving immigrants who join their countryfolk in particular locations, but also those who have been in Australia longer: 'the Vietnamese nucleus in Sydney is now attracting Vietnamese immigrants from other parts of Australia as well as other parts of Sydney' (Webber 1991, p. 22).

However, Hugo (1990, p. 84) cautions that much remains to be researched on the subject of the location of immigrants, particularly the ways in which the settlement patterns of particular birthplace groups change. It is impossible, therefore, to label particular birthplace groups as timelessly dispersed or concentrated. To this list of what needs to be investigated should be added the question of the gender relations, operating within the various waves of immigration of any birthplace group and within the host society at the immigrants' destination, that contribute to determining where male and female immigrants go and after what processes of familial or household negotiation. Madden & Young (1993b), begin to explore this issue. From a survey of 500 immigrants from UK and Ireland, Lebanon, Malaysia and Viet Nam who are currently living in Sydney and Adelaide, it was found that almost half chose their location within Australia because members of their own family lived there, and that this was a more common response among the Lebanese than other birthplace groups, among the Family component immigrants and among the women interviewed. Friends at the chosen location had attracted 16 per cent of the sample—this was consistently more important among the males interviewed, and for the Malaysians and those from UK and Ireland. Possibly worthy of further research was a response on source of information about Australia: 15 per cent of the sample said their spouse provided them with information— a very high proportion of the people making this response were women from all the birthplace groups, except the UK and Ireland one. As the authors of the report say:

> It seems important that for many women a major, if not the sole, source of information about the country they are immigrating to is their spouse. This places a woman in a dependent position in that she has to trust that she would experience life in Australia the way the man perceives it. There is much evidence that this is not the case—that women's and men's settlement experiences can be quite different. (Madden & Young 1993b, p. 117)

Whether the choice of location is one of the issues of information about Australia over which men exercise disproportionate control, was not ascertained.

It seems clear that the set of processes that result in immigrants being concentrated spatially in major metropolitan areas over the last four decades in Australia combine 'formal' opportunities (like jobs or government benefits or services) with 'informal' opportunities (like the knowledge possessed by immigrants' families about how best to obtain access to these formal opportunities). Thus, the labour market of urban areas, as an opportunity set, is accessible to some immigrants more than others because of their 'insider knowledge'; on the other hand, such 'insider knowledge' may blind new immigrants to opportunities that may exist for paid work elsewhere, of which their family 'advisers' are unaware. In characterising the advantages and disadvantages of urban locations for immigrants as potential workplaces, we must combine information about the 'formally' available employment prospects with information about the contacts and 'informal' means accessible to immigrants so they can avail themselves of jobs. It is possible, then, that if immigrants to Australia in the 1950s and 1960s came to Sydney, Melbourne and Adelaide, because these places had developing manufacturing sectors, then subsequent immigrants of the same birthplace group, and even of other birthplace groups, might also select these locations despite a decline in those particular job opportunities.

Employment prospects in settlement locations
What then of the 'formal' employment prospects available to Australia's immigrants in the major cities? (We will consider informal advice and sources of paid work next.) Earlier in the chapter it was shown that people born overseas, especially in NESB countries, are recorded in labour force statistics as highly concentrated in manufacturing industry and in low-skilled occupations there, and also that their levels of occupational attainment are quite low. This picture is echoed in overseas countries. In the 1950s and 1960s in Australia, during what some have characterised as the 'long boom' of economic growth in Western countries:

> the largest cities in Australia, Sydney and Melbourne, experienced the bulk of the industrial growth which was taking place, particularly in manufacturing industries. In the decades following the war, Sydney led the growth in new export-oriented industries such as petrochemicals, metals and paper products. As one of the major foci of industrial expansion, Sydney was also a major port of entry for new immigrants and a large proportion found employment in secondary industry. (Tait & Gibson 1987, p. 5)

During these two post-Second World War decades, relatively high levels of protection for manufacturing industry in Australia were associated with firms that were more labour-intensive than they would have been without such protection (Tait & Gibson 1987, p. 3). The pattern of industry using a sizeable but relatively unskilled labour force was well established by the 1950s:

> this was partly due to the previous colonial status of Australia and a consequent commitment to labour-intensive processing industries, and partly due to the fact that most wartime development had been of import-

replacement industries behind the virtually limitless protection of war-time scarcity and cost-plus financing. Whilst Australia was to remain a high-protection economy, the market conditions of wartime could not persist. Once again, the pressure was for relatively cheap, mobile workers to fit into the spots that already existed, or that would be created as women left the workforce, or were forced out. (Jakubowicz, Morrissey & Palser 1984, p. 21)

Jobs for production workers in manufacturing were thus relatively easy to come by, though trades unions, according to the Jakubowicz, Morrissey and Palser study, (1984, p. 21), favoured Australia-born residents for the better industrial jobs, leaving the other jobs for immigrants. These were jobs in industries in the major Australian cities, for the most part, initiating the location of immigrants because of economic opportunity in those places. Chain migration would cement the spatial pattern.

After the end of the long boom, in the 1970s and 1980s, the economic situations in which immigrants could readily find employment altered. Tait & Gibson (1987, p. 3) argue that, as a reduction in the growth of factory jobs made it more difficult for recent immigrants to find work, so many more have slotted into the economy as self-employed workers, particularly in the retail sector but also in the manufacturing, construction and trade sectors in contract work and outwork. Many immigrants continued to find employment and work in manufacturing, however, because they were directed there by friends and other contacts—even though manufacturing jobs were in shorter supply, many that were taken up were taken up by immigrants in the later post-Second World War decades, and the locations have remained largely urban or suburban. Thus, many immigrants' jobs require them to have access to a busy and large set of production sites, firms and consumers that might demand their labour.

The nature of the jobs available to immigrant women and men clearly affected the characteristics of the work immigrants are recorded officially as doing. It is not clear that these are the sorts of jobs they would have preferred. This is still the case: for example, as Madden and Young (1993b, p. 137) indicate, many Lebanese women in their sample had hoped not to undertake paid work in Australia, believing, if they had families, that their place was in the home and that men should be breadwinners. They also found that women with professional qualifications were more likely to have wanted full-time rather than part-time work on arrival in Australia, and that women from the UK and Ireland in the sample were more interested in part-time or casual work than full-time. In any event, to generalise greatly, what happened in Australia was that when Southern European women arrived in the decades after the Second World War, manu-facturing jobs, usually full-time, were what was available and possible for people without English language competence. When Australia-born women began to enter the labour force in increasing numbers from the 1970s onwards, part-time jobs were on greater offer and part-time jobs are what they largely took up (which caused which is hard to unravel). The argument could probably be advanced that the location of immigrant women in major Australian cities allowed them better access to the labour market and therefore higher participation rates. We dispute this interpretation, however. The higher labour force participation of Australia-born women in recent decades (even outstripping the levels of immigrant women since the late 1980s) is generally attributed to economic want—the declining purchasing power of households with only one income, which makes it more difficult, for example, to purchase a house in a major metropolitan area. Accordingly, it is entirely reasonable to attribute immigrant women's high labour force participation rates in previous decades to economic need, tempered by locational factors which (ironically) made the second income necessary. (This question is argued, in the American context, with respect to high labour force participation by Asian American women (see Wong & Hirschmann 1983; Woo 1985).)

Incorporation of immigrant women and men into particular occupations and industries happens, however, because of a larger number of factors than just the availability of certain jobs in certain places where immigrants happen to be. A less formal channelling occurs, which has been considerably documented in Australian and overseas studies. These channelling processes often make urban labour markets the sites of restriction rather than opportunity for those needing to work for wages. They are processes which actively reinforce the labour market segmentation observed in which NESB immigrants in Australia, particularly women, are found disproportionately in lower-paid and lower-status echelons of the labour market. The processes include: inadequate recognition of immigrants' qualifications and labour force experience by potential employers and referral or counselling institutions (adding to the lack of recognition of women's skills, in general); discrimination, if not in the public sector then in the private sector, which is not so accountable to equal opportunity guidelines; and advice given by a range of informal contacts, including relatives and friends, that might embody stereotypical visions of appropriate immigrant women's and men's work. What is the evidence on these matters?

Adequate recognition of immigrants' skills and experience by potential employers and counselling agencies is very important. The human capital attribute of immigrants just having skills or qualifications is not sufficient to actually reward immigrants with a job. This is not a spatially delimited or primarily a spatially varying matter—but counselling agencies' and employers' practices with regard to qualified immigrants seeking work do occur where the employers and agencies are (largely in large cities) and where the immigrants know to look for work (likewise). Referral is also made to employment prospects in certain locations—no doubt this has been to the industrial areas of major cities because these have housed manufacturing industries.

Non-recognition and non-utilisation of immigrant women's skills by employers is a major factor in the downward mobility these women continue to experience after arrival in Australia. Information about immigrant women's downward occupational mobility (especially if they are of NESB) was presented earlier. The evidence is growing that immigrant women with particular qualifications and experience are not employed at the same level as their Australian counterparts, even after a number of years when their English competence has grown (see, for example, Eliadis, Colanero and Roussos n.d.; PSC 1990). And the evidence has been mounting for a decade: 1981 Census data have been used to show the substantial overall separation rate for immigrants (gender unspecified) from occupations they state they are qualified for in the home country (Department of Immigration File 89/30296, memo to Ms A. Smith, 7 April 1989), and the estimated average annual wastage rate from original occupations.

Accordingly, in July 1989, a National Office of Overseas Skills Recognition (NOOSR) was established by Australia's Federal Government to implement reform strategies for the recognition of immigrants' qualifications and skills. It is described as having a non-discriminatory policy towards recognition of immigrants' skills, and as acknowledging that women often have difficulty entering the work force as recognisably 'skilled' persons (DEET 1990, pp. 13–15).

> Women often face additional problems and delays in having their skills recognised as many arrive as non-principal migrants, that is, either as dependent spouses or children, and do not necessarily have their qualifications assessed as part of the migration process. (DEET 1990, p. 14)

We have referred to this matter earlier as one of the inadequacies, from a gender equity point of view, associated with the allocation of one person (usually a male) in an immigrating family/household to the status of Principal Applicant.

Mitchell, Tait and Castles (1990) indicate that professionally qualified immigrants in Australia do use the Federal Government's employment service, unlike the women interviewed by Alcorso (1991). (However, the Mitchell, Tait and Castles study does not single out women in its discussion of job search strategies.) In particular, those with professional overseas qualifications use the Government's Professional Employment Service (PES); but the outcome of this use of the Government's service seems unsatisfactory in the case of professionals, as it does in the case of those without such qualifications: Mitchell, Tait and Castles (1990) found that people with considerable professional work experience overseas spent longer periods unemployed on arrival than those with less experience. (This disparity was especially true of those without good English.) The authors surmise that not only do employers see those with more experience as overqualified for positions available but also they found that PES staff pushed qualified immigrants to take any job they could: 'PES officials interviewed confirmed the claim made by many survey respondents that PES staff encouraged jobless professionals to take "any job" to get Australian work experience' (Mitchell, Tait & Castles 1990, p. 65). Despite this advice, the resulting job searches were generally unsuccessful.

When asked about their experience of immigration to Australia, and how they felt about what had happened to them in their employment circumstances, many of those surveyed by Mitchell, Tait and Castles reported utter personal devastation. They felt great resentment at the information they had been given before arrival in Australia, about the prospects for professionals here. They also felt that they had little hope of achieving a suitable job in Australia when employers were permitted to call for 'local experience' (even if overseas experience in that profession is almost identical to what work experience would be in Australia) before appointing someone to a job —immigrants having no possibility of gaining local experience before arrival.

These experiences of professionals finding work and being allocated to jobs that are less than they expected, are reported also in the international literature. Ng (1988) has described how immigrant women attending a government-sponsored employment agency in Canada were channelled through the procedures of the agency into jobs thought 'suitable' for immigrant women, despite their previous experiences and qualifications. These allocations of the women relied on a common social construction of immigrant women. There is some anecdotal indication, however, from professional immigrants interviewed by Mitchell, Tait and Castles (1990, p. 119) that the 'closed shop' nature of Australian professions, and the way this is permitted by the Australian Government, is not as severe in 'the more open systems of Canada or the US where they [immigrants] would be given an opportunity to prove themselves'. Misztal (1991, p. 55) makes this point too, from stories of other immigrants.

It cannot be claimed that the experiences of professionals or women from different birthplace groups in seeking and finding work are primarily spatially influenced. Several issues could be followed up, however, to indicate the rootedness of employment cultures in particular places and locations, with respect to institutional behaviours such as lack of recognition of immigrants' qualifications, the apparent inappropriateness of government job-search agencies for many immigrant women or the behaviours of immigrants themselves as they look for work. These issues include spatially dependent matters like: the degree to which immigrant women are limited in their job searches to particular places, because of child care or other needs that cannot be satisfied if they work further away from their homes;

and whether or not there is an urban bias in the advice given to immigrant women by job placement personnel, as part of the stereotypes about where 'ethnic' women normally work or because of ignorance of employment prospects in rural towns or communities (most government and other employment advisers being in larger towns and cities).

Actual discrimination by employers against immigrants is intentional exclusion of immigrants from employment. It is hard to prove (see Foster, Marshall & Williams 1991, p. xv), not least because immigrant women are less likely to use the provisions of the state to seek redress in cases where racial or sexual discrimination has occurred and therefore to have evidence of discrimination against them assessed in the public gaze. In the State of Victoria, NESB immigrant women are less likely than men or Anglo women to seek the assistance of ombudsmen or other provisions for making rights-based claims (Rayner 1992). International evidence suggests that discrimination must occur in labour markets in which immigrant women fare so poorly (Grossman 1984, p. 349). Glenn (1986), for example, demonstrates the subtleties of the labour market segmentation process for Japanese American women in the United States.

If immigrant women are positively channelled in the direction of certain employment sectors and locations by members of their informal networks—relatives and friends—rather than counsellors in the private or public sectors, then we may level the charge of discrimination or unintentional suppression of prospects far less readily. Indeed, the availability of paid employment in the 'ethnic economy', as outwork or as wage labour, may be a reason why immigrants choose the locations they do—especially at times of recession in which rapid pathways to other employment are limited (international studies examining this issue include Anthias 1983; Morokvasic 1981, 1991). It is also true that women, whether immigrant or not, under the stress of difficult economic times may redefine their homes as workplaces for more than purely domestic labour, hence altering the relations between home work, conventionally termed 'domestic duties' and wage earning. Nor is work in family businesses always oppressive: Lever-Tracy (1992) has shown how successful immigrant women managers of family businesses in Australia can be.

The place-based nature of the channelling of immigrant women into certain jobs, and the discrimination (if it can be demonstrated) that precludes them from other opportunities, consists in the way that social relations of class, gender and ethnicity characterise employment relations in certain destination locations. Immigrants from a particular location, if their class, gender or ethnicity is interpreted in the destination as unlike those of their employers (in government institutions, or businesses, or homes as sites of domestic employment) may experience discrimination or reduced employment prospects. Radcliffe (1990, p. 381), in a different context, makes this point in referring to the relations of power in the domestic employment of women immigrants in Peruvian households, noting 'their genesis in a hierarchical class society, divided by wealth, ethnicity and regional differences'.

In Australia, the immigrant population is perhaps too diverse for discrimination by Australian employers to occur on the basis of immigrants' precise region of origin. Historical research could uncover, however, whether employers' activities have effectively stereotyped immigrants as regional groupings that are socially and economically disparaged. Such actions with respect to immigrants might characterise the social relations of certain Australian places rather than others. It would be a research project of great interest that compared the incorporation of immigrants into the labour markets and social institutions of different Australian localities, and the local ideologies about class and ethnicity that this mobilised.

Consider now the informal networks through which immigrant women gain access to 'insider knowledge' of Australian life, in destinations where other immigrants live. We have noted already that 'insider knowledge' can facilitate settlement, as newly arrived immigrants learn from their friends or community contacts the way 'things work', or what might be different in any avenue of life from the immigrant's origin situation. Considerable information on the significance of insider knowledge for immigrants arriving in Australia exists about the process of job search—going about finding 'appropriate' employment. Rush and Steen (1987) describe how the sixty-eight Spanish-speaking women they interviewed in Melbourne had mostly found their jobs through word-of-mouth contacts, rather than through the Commonwealth Employment Service (CES) or advertisements in newspapers. Alcorso (1991, p. 62) found the same thing:

> It seems that by far the most common means of finding a job was through the assistance of a friend or a relative in one's own ethnic community. Often, women had *sought* work using a variety of means—looking in newspapers, asking people they knew, using the Commonwealth Employment Service etc. What was interesting, however, was the means by which they had actually *found* their respective jobs. The majority of women found their first and second jobs through someone they knew, and a large proportion also found their third and fourth jobs this way. In a typical situation a relative, or sometimes a friend, of the unemployed woman helped her obtain a job in the same workplace where the relative or friend was employed. This was true of the long settled women as well as of those newly arrived.

Alcorso reported that women she interviewed had actually been asked by their employers to find other women to join the firm. And she found very marked the lack of success of the women in finding work through the CES. At times when factory work was available in

Australia, immigrant women without English competence or qualifications were able to be incorporated into manufacturing work through the efforts of their friends and relatives already at work in these situations.

Fincher, Campbell and Webber (1993) also provide information on this subject, describing the stories of a number of recently arrived immigrants in Melbourne, in which the various sources of advice sought and received by the immigrants are evident. Insider knowledge, it appears from this study, can channel women into a limited range of employment situations deemed appropriate by other family members and able to be achieved in the difficult circumstances of new settlement. (This knowledge and advice *does* result in paid employment, so it has this advantage, even if the employment is more limited than the full range of job opportunities that might be, in theory, available.) Examples of advice about 'appropriate' or obtainable work and its effect of channelling immigrant women into particular lines of work that they as individuals may not prefer, are numerous Vietnamese women interviewed who slotted rapidly after arrival into piece-work sewing at home, following advice by family members; some Lebanese household groups began to arrange to lease small corner stores (milk bars), following family members and Lebanese friends in this. (This is congruent with evidence by Hassan, Healy and McKenna (1985, p. 181) that 'emigrants from Lebanon are generally assured of migrant kin support and some form of job or economic protection in a new country'.)

The use of insider knowledge by newly arrived immigrants clearly depends on the proximity of those immigrants to a group of advice-givers who are part of the social relations of a particular place, and know how to operate to achieve certain ends (for example, finding a job) in that specific location. The production and use of insider information, then, is a spatially rooted and restricted phenomenon.

Incorporation into paid work that is not officially recorded, that is part of the so-called 'black economy', is also an experience of some immigrant women that depends on insider advice and knowledge about the opportunities for such work that exist in particular places. The fact that this activity is not recorded means it is not regulated and protected by whatever government safeguards exist. Contributing to a topic that is enormously hard to document and sensitive to discuss, Knowles (1985) has described three types of employment in which Vietnamese women in Perth participated between 1978 and 1984, giving reasons through case studies for the access to these types of employment. The first is permanent official employment. This is what is best described in the official statistics. Knowles notes that very few Vietnamese refugees gain access to this type of employment. Casual, semi-official employment is the second type—it is often in factories, market gardens and restaurants, from which workers are often fired when business is slow. Pay can be low and conditions exploitative. This type of employment is 'semi-official', because neither boss nor worker openly acknowledges it. Home-based unofficial employment is the third type of employment. Small businesses run from the home include child care, sewing, cooking, vegetable growing and hairdressing. Sewing is especially popular, not only for private clients but for retail firms who deliver goods to be sewn as piece-work. The pay per item is low, but women who produce a lot can earn good wages. Women who undertake this work find it advantageous because it is largely tax-free, does not require English competence and can be accommodated alongside other activities like child care. Knowles estimates that about one-third of all the Vietnamese households in Perth operate a household business of this sort.

Knowles reasons that because of their gender (which meant that in Viet Nam they were often uneducated), their ethnicity (which means they cannot speak English) and their poverty as refugees, these women have few employment options and often find themselves in unofficial outwork as a result.

Other evidence comes from a survey of women in New South Wales doing paid work at home (NSW Department of Industrial Relations and Employment 1987), in which 40 per cent of respondents generally spoke a language other than English. This survey focused on women doing three types of homework—clothing outwork, paid child care at home and freelance work in journalism and publishing. Of these three work types, women of NESB were significantly represented only among the seventy-eight clothing outworkers interviewed. Nearly all the women had small children of their own or grandchildren to look after as they worked; this, in the absence of affordable child care and transport services, was the main reason for working like this at home.

On the other hand, some women, also immigrant outworkers in Sydney, felt that such an employment arrangement reconciled being in paid work with having children (Neuman & Elder 1982, p. 8). Vietnamese women outworkers in Melbourne are reported similarly (Lam, Luong & Cahill 1989).

Whatever the significance of this work arrangement for immigrant women, we can make two points about it. First, it is an employment arrangement that relies on insider advice and knowledge of paid work opportunities that are not evident through publicised channels like the media and government employment services; it is a spatially bounded and rooted phenomenon and one, it could be hypothesised, that is more likely to occur in major cities. Secondly, the fact that women must undertake such work in order to accommodate their child-caring and income-generation needs is an indictment of government policies that purport to support women in the paid labour force through provision of affordable and appropriate child-care services. Undertaking outwork is hardly a way to avoid the double burden of domestic and paid labour: rather it mixes the two burdens up in the same location through a long, interminable day. As Martin pointed out some years ago now:

> outwork, located in the home away from a legitimate workplace and workplace activities, where the wife/mother is forced to work without relinquishing any of her 'domestic' responsibilities, is possibly the most extreme and punitive statement of our society's reluctance to reconcile these two spheres [of production and social reproduction]. (Martin 1984, p. 115)

Raising the point of the intertwining of immigrant women's domestic and paid work, and how child-care needs must often be accommodated by undertaking paid piece-work in the home, brings us to the issue of settlement services for immigrant women. We have chosen to concentrate in particular on language and child-care services, because these seem crucially represented in immigrant women's statements about their settlement needs. Of course, there are also many other services (like care of elderly dependants of immigrants and legal and health services) that could also be considered here. The question being considered about the services, then, is: How are they accessible to immigrant women in different places? This includes considering whether they take a more accessible form in different places, or a range of forms able to be chosen from.

Child care and language services

The use of government-supported child care, or access to it, by immigrant women in Australia, particularly those of NESB, has been described in a number of studies (for example, Yeatman 1988) and government documents (for example, DEET 1990). A recent survey in Victoria found that only 7 per cent of the child-care places it identified involved 'parents with a low degree of English language competency'. It noted the results of an earlier national survey in which 83 per cent of family units which had at least one parent born in a non-English-speaking country used informal rather than formal child-care arrangements (Victorian Department of Labour 1989, p. 75). Whether these figures represent lack of access to child care for economic or locational reasons, or failure to take up child-care places because the services available are culturally inappropriate, is of course unclear from these figures. Lower rates of use of child-care services by immigrant women may also be due to the facts that immigrant women may work shifts in disproportionately high numbers, at times when many child-care services are unavailable, and that immigrant women homeworkers largely care for their children at home, with informal help as necessary from friends and relatives. There are activists, advocating child care of different forms and philosophies, who claim that non-Anglo women in Australia find provisions here inappropriate, and are unwilling to have their children spend long periods with strangers:

> This is an acknowledged reality. But because the 'specialness' requires a different approach, untried and unknown to many of the predominantly Anglo-Australian bureaucrats and service providers, child care services for families from NESB are often reduced to the provision of workers from NESB, who introduce the existing concepts and services to the families, in their own language, of course. (D'Mello 1990, p. 3)

There will clearly be diversity between immigrant women as to their views on the suitability of child care, and their economic and spatial access to child-care services. There are also great variations in the level and form of child-care provisions in different places. In Melbourne, for example, child-care places are more numerous in the inner city than the outer municipalities, the product of at least one decade's attempts by older suburban municipalities to channel federal funds for child-care into their localities. Even within those municipalities to which federal funding for child care has been available for some time, however, there is variation in the level of provision and its form, and in its accessibility to a range of social groups that are not of the Anglo, middle income, nine-to-five weekday working, characteristics.

If this is the situation in our major cities, in which immigrant women have been paid labour force participants in many localities for many years now, over a time when federal funding for child-care schemes has been available, then what happens in rural areas or country towns? In rural areas, immigrant women are likely to have fewer relatives or people from the same birthplace or region to help with child-care needs. If they wish to attend language or other courses, this becomes a pressing problem. Mageean (1990, p. 30), in a study documenting the needs of rural immigrant women if they are to gain access to courses in TAFE colleges, emphasises that:

> Child care is a vital issue in immigrant women's access and participation in TAFE. Often these women come from cultures in which there is a large extended family to care for the children. In isolated rural Australian communities, however, they may have no one to help them. Furthermore, in some cultures it is unacceptable for women to ask their husbands to mind the children while they attend class. So without child care these women are in practice excluded from TAFE.

Gray et al. (1991, p. xiv) confirm that services directly suited to or appropriate for NESB immigrants 'are sparse, largely due to rural centres' inability to generate the "critical mass" of potential clients demanded by agencies'. Their study of immigrant settlement in country areas focused on five country towns in New South Wales and Queensland, and interviewed over a hundred immigrants, the majority of whom were women (though this fact is not emphasised.) For ethnic groups represented in Australia in small numbers, of course, location in a rural area presents even greater problems when services are needed (Jupp, McRobbie & York 1991, p. 34; Foster & Rado 1991). As well, the same Anglocentrism claimed to characterise urban child-care services is claimed for the range of rural settlement services, in that service providers are largely unaware of immigrants' specific needs (Gray et al. 1991). Though ethno-specific services were noted not to exist in Wagga Wagga (NSW), one of the sites studied, the immigrants interviewed were quite aware of the child care provided in the town. Child care ranked with CES and the Department of Social Security (DSS) among the services of which they were most aware, and they indicated they would readily use the service (Gray et al. 1991, pp. 19–20). This appears to contradict the claims of some advocates of appropriate child care for immigrants.

On the other hand, in another of Gray et al's case studies, in which the location and birthplace groups of the immigrants interviewed differed from the first case mentioned, 'there was considerable variety in awareness of services' and the interviewers felt that 'cultural factors would . . . predispose many away from using some of the services' (p. 33). Whether child care was among the services found culturally inappropriate in this area by the immigrants interviewed is not clear from the data presented. In yet another case study (for Tumut, NSW), child care was one of the services of which most immigrants interviewed were aware, yet most stated they would only use services if family and friends could not help (Gray et al. 1991, p. 66).

The point is clear that propensity to use or reject services (including child care) whose cultural characteristics differ from one's own varies between different immigrant groups. As well, however, government-sponsored child-care services are scarcer in rural than urban areas, so the chance of finding an appropriate service is smaller. Though we have noted that most immigrants to Australia have gone to major cities, and many women among them have worked in both home and paid workplace, it is the case that if immigrant women in rural areas sought to work or train outside the home, government child-care services would probably be unavailable to them.

> Lack of resources and the critical mass problem were raised consistently by agencies. Immigrant-specific services are at best rare in rural areas. Some services used by immigrants have been closed in recent years. Where services are offered, they cannot be provided at the same standard as offered in the major urban centres. The inability to stream language classes is perhaps the best illustration.

So conclude Gray et al. (1991, p. 95) about all the towns and services they examined. Consider now English language classes.

Access to English language classes is of major importance to settlement for all immigrants. Women, however, seem often to have more limited effective access to these services than do immigrant men. Perhaps this is because they spend so much time settling their families in the early months or years in Australia, or sometimes because the values of their cultures and households preclude their participation in language classes that take particular formats (for example, are coeducational, or occur at night, or require absence from small children). The 1991 national conference on Migrant Women, Settlement and Training (hosted and primarily organised by the South Australian Migrant Women's Working Centre) not only provided a platform for a range of speakers with expertise and practical experience in this field, but also presented information drawn from a wide-ranging consultation with NESB women nationally. One of the aims of the consultation was to document the requirements of immigrant and refugee women in relation to access to English language training. The findings of these consultations bear out the claims made in this section.

It is important to note that the Federal Government is making considerable effort to deal with the needs of immigrant women for language training and to overcome particular problems for such women. For example, the Adult Migrant Education Program (AMEP) National Plan 1991-92 lists the following among its objectives and strategies (based on personal communication with DILGEA in 1992):

1.1.1 (a) reserve 10% of program resources for people with more than 5 years residence, concentrating on courses for migrants at work or for people (particularly women) who did not participate in the program earlier due to family responsibilities;

1.1.2 (b) enrol at least 75% of new arrivals with limited or no proficiency in English within 12 months of arrival (70% in 1989) and 85% within 2 years of arrival including strategies for women to access the program sooner . . .

2.3.2 (b) use tutor support as a means of reaching isolated people (particularly women) including those who have been in Australia for more than 5 years but who have not accessed the AMEP for family or related cultural reasons . . .

4.4.1 Facilitate attendance of parents, particularly women, at AMEP English learning arrangements through provision of child care support at convenient locations, in accord with overall objectives of the program.

There is considerable evidence that many immigrant women do not access official English language and literacy programs and of those who do, many do not achieve at levels which will significantly enhance their prospects in the world of paid work (see the bibliography in Foster and Rado (1991)). Some comments arising from the direct experience of immigrant women (as recorded in the consultations for the 1991 national conference on Migrant Women's Settlement and Training) crystallise the gap between planning and delivery which many policy-makers, it was felt, do not comprehend:

they were continually negotiating the *choices* between family life, employment and English language training.

the women also made the observations that the comments made between them, spanning a period of time of between 1 and 17 years, revealed that the situation had not significantly improved in this time.

getting children organised and travelling a long way means you are exhausted by the time you get to class.

shopping list for groceries etc. are unnecessary because you can just go and buy off the shelf in the supermarket—whereas knowing how to speak to the officers at the DSS, CES or hospital is important.

In the beginning I couldn't attend classes because of the children . . . my husband went to classes because he thought it would help him find work. My work was to stay home and look after the baby and make the food. For that I didn't need English. When my baby went to school I did the same for my second child.

I made a mistake—I had a baby.

there is no link between the context of the course with my qualifications and desired employment.

we were told you should go to class and lose your accent then you'll get a job.

we should be able to learn English when we need it, not when someone else has decided we can.

How does access to language services vary between different places, in particular between major metropolitan centres and rural areas? Much of the information used in the above discussion of child care and services generally applies in the case of language services. Organisers and teachers of English literacy classes in Victorian country towns, for example, have claimed that small, isolated communities do not yield classes of sufficient size (Foster & Rado 1991).

How do government language programs cater to immigrant women, as opposed to men? The AMEP is the major government-funded program to teach English to adult immigrants. As implied above, subsidised language training is available to newly arrived immigrants, with greatest priority being given to the first two years of settlement period, followed by the period up to five years of settlement and then some provision for those whose residence period is greater than five years. It is obvious from the reasons identified by women themselves that such a policy will disadvantage many women whose family responsibilities and need to juggle home and paid work responsibilities in the early stages of settlement (taking advantage of the 'insider knowledge' provided by speakers of their native languages) entail a double burden such that they do not 'choose' to undertake language classes. They are in fact penalised for their contribution to Australian society as mothers and paid workers.

AMEP classes are provided in a range of settings in metropolitan areas, including formal classes run by the state-based Adult Migrant Education Service (AMES), TAFE colleges, university language units, Intensive Language Learning Centres, Ministry of Education programs and the less formal classes to be found in locations such as neighbourhood houses, women's learning centres and community health centres. There are English in the Workplace programs and many skills-based courses with a language component, such as SkillShare, to be found also in a range of settings. It is not possible to duplicate this wide range in all country centres. Classes of the AMEP are provided in country towns, especially by the TAFE sector. For many women (in both urban and rural areas), mainstream courses may be forbidding because of the complex rules associated with entry to the courses and the relatively formal institutional nature of their format. Those who have had low levels of education in their own countries, and especially the women who are not literate in their mother tongue, face special handicaps in accessing English literacy and basic education courses. Where English language classes can be held in local neighbourhood houses, their informal, women-only characteristics may make them more accessible to some immigrant women. Those courses providing bilingual support services are also likely to be more attractive to immigrant women. The Home Tutor Scheme developed with the AMEP is another device used to cater for house-bound immigrant women. One of the difficulties for this program in country areas is the limited range of appropriate volunteers, the difficulty of providing them with adequate training and the actual language gain made by women in the program—too low in many cases for the participants to be confident of using their English in work settings should they wish to. In spite of continual improvement in language services, their nature, provision and outcomes are bedevilled by many limitations, among which the locational factor plays an important part. It is, of course, a moot point whether a sufficient level of resources could ever be provided from the public purse to service the language needs of immigrants adequately, whether in metropolitan or rural centres, given the diversity of needs within Australia's continuing immigrant and refugee flows.

When considering two major government settlement initiatives that are of special significance to women—child care (to ease the pressure due to domestic and paid labour, or at least to make this dual load easier to accomplish) and English language training (to allow the fullest participation in all aspects of the host society), two points become clear. First, the form in which these services are presented is not always appropriate to all immigrant women. And secondly, the fullest range of the services is present only in metropolitan areas. From the standpoint of gender equity, women are disadvantaged by the inappropriateness of child care, because it is they who will have to make alternative, informal child-care arrangements, or else have no choice but to remain at home when they may not always have wished for this. In addition, women are disadvantaged if they have less access to English language training, and their isolation within their own home and language group is increased.

Conclusion

In this chapter we have considered one major settlement issue for immigrant women—participation in the paid labour force—its gender equity implications, and the contribution of the state to this situation. From statistical and qualitative accounts we have documented the 'double burden' that immigrant women have commonly carried in the post-Second World War years, this consisting of their engagement in paid work and unpaid domestic work, the former at higher levels for NESB immigrant women and under worse conditions than other labour market groupings.

There are ways in which immigration policies have contributed directly to the low labour force status of many immigrant women. The difficulties for the partners of Principal Applicants in having their qualifications and work experience recognised soon after arrival, is one direct matter. Settlement services like child care and language training, in so far as they are inappropriate to the different requirements of immigrant women, are also areas in which the state has a direct role in producing conditions conducive to double burdens for women that are more irksome than they need be.

Overall, however, our conclusion is that the disadvantage occurring to many immigrant women because of the extended paid labour force commitments and family duties they have had no choice but to assume are, rather, an *indirect* product of immigration policy. The double burden outcome arose because of the precise locations in which employment was available at the times the Australian Government was admitting large numbers of immigrants—these places were metropolitan, and so housing costs (in particular) often required two incomes (especially if those incomes were relatively low).

Of course, it is true that most immigrants must work hard to establish themselves anywhere in the early years of settlement. Our point, however, is that locational circumstances made the income required even larger than might otherwise have been the case. It is also true that we are invoking a responsibility for government, here, without allowing our gaze to shift within immigrant households, and to ask if immigrant men were alleviating that double burden on their partners. As with any feminist discussion of the way women manage their various commitments, it goes without saying that gender equity will be dramatically improved if domestic responsibilities, child care, and so on, are shared.

Chapter 5: Conclusion—immigration, gender equity and policy

The aggregate figures on numbers of men and women entering Australia as immigrants in the last decade give no cause for concern that either women or men are massively underrepresented. Numbers of men and women arriving have long been approximately equal, with variations in the totals due to matters like the stages of the immigration waves entering from different countries. This last chapter, however, looks past the total immigrant numbers and poses questions about the material presented in chapters 2, 3 and 4, that derive from the gender equity concepts aired in chapter 1. In this exercise the gendering processes underlying the total immigrant numbers arriving in Australia (like the links between marriage and immigration), the components of the immigrant intake (like the Department of Immigration's selection categories) and their implications, in terms of which men and women are selected to immigrate, and the gender-specific settlement outcomes of the immigration experience, will be looked at. To what degree are the situations described in the previous chapters the product of policies that have been deficient in the formulations of gender equity on which they have been based?

Before identifying once more the criteria that have been isolated to help develop questions about gender equity, it should be clear what this chapter is *not* aiming for. The chapter is not seeking to identify a long list of specific policy recommendations, ranging right across the many levers of immigration and settlement policy for negotiation about ready take-up and implementation. Rather, it is intended to raise some different ways of thinking about immigration policy matters, prompted by viewing the material in chapters 2 to 4 through the lens of the gender equity criteria selected, that might help find new directions in policy. An important point to note, as well, is that the comments will be about policy *processes* as well as policy *outcomes*: like many perspectives on social justice more generally, our view of gender justice is that it comprises adequate representation of diverse gender groups in information and decision-making about their circumstances, as much as it comprises pre-specified outcomes about those circumstances.

The criteria used to (re)view the material of chapters 2 to 4, then, are those specified in chapter 1:

1. the degree to which policies take seriously the identified differences of their constituents and make amends for the disadvantages associated with those differences, in ways that do not require elimination of the differences;

2. the degree to which the voices of disadvantaged social groups, formed by affinity rather than by bureaucratic categorisation, are sought, heard and taken into account in the policy-making process.

Criterion 1 is considered an *outcomes-oriented* criterion and criterion 2 is concerned with *process*. Furthermore, it is suggested that a condition needed for the satisfactory consideration of gender equity in policy and policy processes is that those policies and processes are continually scrutinised—that there should be both a concerted conceptual gaze on, and a frequent detailed evaluation of, particular policies and their implementation. The rest of the discussion is structured around these two criteria and one condition for gender equity. Selected examples are taken from the previous chapters to illustrate our thinking on these questions.

Allowing for diversity and difference in policy prescriptions

When the degree to which tolerance (even encouragement) of diversity and difference is present in immigration policies and practices is considered, the question being asked is how immigrant men and women are envisaged in ways that might make a difference in their access to immigration. The obvious place to begin exploring this question is the immigration selection categories, with one of whose standards prospective Principal Applicants must comply if they are to immigrate to Australia. It is clear that the stereotypical attribution of certain qualities to men and women wanting to immigrate has declined in the decades since the 1950s (see chapter 2); reduction in the discretion of those officers selecting immigrants is also evident. Avowedly gender-neutral policies now pertain, which may, however, still retain some biases in the ways that masculinity and femininity are associated with particular desired or undesired characteristics of potential immigrants.

Quite apart from the manner in which contemporary policy prescriptions are interpreted by government officials (especially immigration officers overseas), do the selection categories still presume certain types of immigrants in the way they define their eligibility criteria? Figures have been seen in the previous chapters to indicate how women (for example) are disproportionately represented in family-oriented categories and men in skill-oriented categories. It was also estimated that across the Skill, Family and Humanitarian components at least 40 per cent of female settler arrivals to Australia were accompanying wives or married or engaged; far more females than males are 'accompanying spouses' in the Skill category. Marital status is clearly far more important in immigration for women than for men. Skill attributes seem to be more important in the selection of men.

Several questions arise from this when gender equity criteria are used as a means of organisation. The first has to do with the masculinist interpretation of skill, which continues to define immigration skills categories and associated selection judgments. The second relates to the correlation between marriage and immigration, especially for women, and whether this is a gender equity issue. A third relates to the designation of one person in a family unit as the Principal Applicant, which thereby relegates other adults in the group to a lesser status.

There has been discussion of the ways in which selection for immigration under the Skill category is based on interpretations of skill that can be of disadvantage to women. This is one reason, we allege, why women are represented less in entry figures associated with this category—it is easier for them to comply with requirements for entry under the family-oriented selection criteria, often by virtue of their marital status. If skill-based preference is given to immigrants, then the definitions of skill deployed need to be re-examined so as to include those skills that more often characterise women, and women need to be encouraged to acknowledge and define their skills. While the move to include people's competencies as well as their qualifications in immigration selection partly addresses this concern, it is important to ensure that what are defined as 'competencies' and ranked as the most desirable competencies are not also those more often found in men.

Women enter Australia more often under the family-oriented selection criteria. Indeed, it has been claimed that if family immigration is cut back, the numbers of women able to immigrate will decline. (The same argument has been made to justify the continuation of the scheme under which women enter Canada as domestic labourers, and have fewer citizenship rights in so doing than other classes of immigrant there.) Similarly, it has been one interpretation that recent growth in the family categories has been of advantage to women. This poses a dilemma, for it may be that entry under the family criteria, which demands of women compliance with rules associated with their marital status, causes difficulty for certain women in gaining immigrant entry or in the settlement process. The question here, then, is whether the entry of women primarily under rules associated with their marital status is equitable, and if it is not, would cutting it be more inequitable? There is some indirect evidence that single women have greater difficulty immigrating to Australia than married women—for example the assumed high proportion of illegal immigrants who are single women—and that constraining women to enter Australia largely through their family and marital connections (their relationship, in particular, to men) means that women without those relationships may lose out. Singleness is not a good attribute if you are an 'unskilled' (by definition) woman seeking immigration to Australia. Neither is gay or lesbian sexuality: the definitions of spouse under the *Migration Act* and Regulations preclude spouses of the same sex. If the emphasis in immigration selection were moved away from family criteria, or particularly from its marital component, as this is what affects many women most directly, there would, of course, need to be accompanying policy efforts to ensure that other categories were amended specifically to include diverse groups of women in the immigrant intake, in ways that non-marital categories currently fail to do.

When applications are made for immigration to Australia, one person in the household or family group concerned is nominated as Principal Applicant. This is an administrative device. Most often, for a range of reasons which have been mentioned in the text, men are designated Principal Applicant. It is generally claimed by administrators of this system that it makes no difference to subsequent settlement prospects who in a family grouping is identified as the Principal Applicant—and the Australian arrangement is better in this regard than other countries where the 'prime' member of an immigrant household is entitled to better settlement services than other adult 'dependants'. However, there is a likelihood that the administrative method of choosing one immigrant as Principal Applicant, usually a male, may lead to a lag in recognition of the (usually female) accompanying adult immigrant's qualifications in Australia, this in turn probably resulting in a longer period of unemployment for that accompanying immigrant. This issue is recounted in greater detail below. It raises the matter for policy scrutiny, however, of whether adult members of an immigrant household should be so differentiated in the administrative treatment they receive, as gender injustice may, quite unintentionally, be one result.

Encouraging equitable processes

Equitable processes are just as important as equitable outcomes, and often are the central determinant of just outcomes. We are asking here whether the policies and practices of immigration and settlement have been grounded in efforts to seek out diverse and different social groups, encouraging their heterogeneity and ensuring their status in the determination of outcomes. Dealing with equitable processes in the practice of immigrant selection is difficult, for it raises the issue of whether the Australian state should accord participatory status in its decision-making to non-nationals, citizens of other countries applying for entry here and being 'selected' by the Australian state. This issue of broader global social justice is not part of the brief here. There are several points that emerge from this study, however, about the processes through which diverse immigrants interact with the Australian Government.

The first discussion point concerns the question of whether or not women (in particular) benefit from immigration to Australia. This has been a concern through all the preceding chapters, especially chapter 4, where immigrant women's shouldering of the 'double burden' of paid and unpaid work in Australia was described. Based on the international and Australian evidence and literature, it does appear that women migrating as settlers to First World countries have often been disadvantaged by the experience relative to what their circumstances might have been had they not migrated, and certainly relative to their expectations. They also seem disadvantaged, often, in comparison with their male counterparts. Great diversity according to such things as class, age and the match of language group to that in the host country must, of course, qualify this gross generalisation.

It seems that if women are so often the losers in the immigration experience in a range of ways, would not an immigration policy based in gender equity be one that seeks to engage potential women immigrants in discussion about this, to generate more complex information for and with them about the immigration process in ways they could most readily accommodate? It seems that a more equitable *process* of ensuring that information is available to women seeking to immigrate would be, for example, for information exchange to occur through networks of contacts for potential immigrant women with their counterparts in Australia. Those counterparts would be people of similar background and position, but not bureaucrats, and preferably not family members, who might feel obliged to hide the bleaker aspects of immigration in encouraging their family members to join them. It seems particularly important that individual, potential immigrant women be encouraged to participate in such information generation when there is evidence from the Madden and Young (1993b) study that for many women most of the information about the country they are migrating to comes from their spouses! If prospective immigrant women could separately interact with a network of women like them, who had gone before, then the immigration *process* in which they engaged would be more gender-equitable in allowing them (at least) information and participation that respected their difference, no matter what the final outcomes of it might be in terms of the women's immigration decision.

Another similar point emerges as a general response to the varying evidence described in chapter 4 about NESB women's frequent lack of participation and lack of advantage in the important sphere of paid work. There is a clear demand for the organisational structures that have bearing on this sphere of daily life to seek out groups of difference and insist that the views of such groups be heard through the establishment of appropriate consultative mechanisms. The relevant organisations are not just those of government, like the Commonwealth Employment Service (CES), which are so often thought to be channelling immigrants into stereotyped occupational vacancies. They are also, for example, organisations like unions, community groups for women (who must respond to gender difference), and those organisations responsible for the 'closed shop' nature of Australian professions. This perhaps raises the possibility of an enhanced role for the settlement agencies of the Australian state, to extend their work more strongly in the direction of advocacy of proper processes to cement the place and the views of people of different attributes, and different identifications. As is clear, however, from discussions of, for example, the frequent lack of recognition of immigrants' qualifications by employers, there is only so far that direct government regulation of outcomes can go in achieving gender justice. The existence of proper participatory processes, where no particular outcome is guaranteed, is a further step in respecting difference.

Gender equity requires continued scrutiny

If policies and practices are really to reach better levels of gender equity, ongoing examination is required, both of the overall philosophy to which particular policies and practices respond and of the details of policy implementation that may exclude particular groups. We will make one point about a major exercise in conceptual scrutiny which we feel is needed, and then pose a couple of scenarios which show the sort of detailed examination of policy practice required if diverse gender groups are to be justly accommodated.

There is need for a major conceptual review of the way that marriage serves immigration aims. How may marriage and immigration continue to be linked, without boxing immigrant women in to marital relationships (instead of being single) in order to immigrate here, with the occasional attendant problems of domestic gender violence in change-of-status situations that have been the great concern of Australian immigrant women's groups in the last few years? There is here an important and basic question: Why does Australian immigration policy and practice rely so heavily on marital relationships—must it always do so, and what conceptual underpinnings have caused it to do so to date? If marriage and immigration are cemented together in current immigration law and policy, is this a pragmatic decision, taken in order to identify most readily the groupings of people who may accompany any individual applicant? Further, if the link between marriage and immigration policy continues to be so significant, is there any way that gender inequity can be rooted out of immigration policy? The gender injustices now associated with the marriage and immigration link include heterosexism, and the apparent disadvantage (of which there are only hints to date) experienced by women in many situations where marriage–immigration links are used 'creatively' to gain entry to Australia—in scams, frauds and some situations in which Australian citizens procure overseas partners.

Considering how a link between marriage and immigration could be maintained, but without the associated gender inequities, it was mentioned earlier that the immigration selection categories could be 'freed up' in their accessibility to women; this might decrease women's reliance on marriage-related entry requirements. But much of the marriage-related injustices experienced by vulnerable immigrant women once in Australia may occur in the marital home. So there is a broader issue here of the degree to which the state can and will actually regulate the domestic affairs of heterosexual married couples. In the case of serial sponsorship by male Australian citizens of Filipino women, for example, will it limit the right of those male citizens to engage in serial sponsorship if the practice is detrimental to the women concerned, or will the Government stay out of these 'domestic' affairs with the argument that it is a right of Australians to marry whomever they choose and however often they are legally able? It seems ironic that governments rely so heavily on the institution of marriage to select immigrants, and yet are less willing or less effective in intervening in the unfortunate domestic consequences of this for some women. There is need for some conceptual scrutiny, then, of the purposes for which immigration is linked to marriage in Australia, and of the gender inequity that may be associated with the state's use of the 'private' sphere for this purpose when it fails to tackle or even acknowledge the 'private' problems for women that may result. After all, marriage is not always entered into entirely for reasons of personal choice—there are structural inequities associated with the institution of marriage. If governments are 'hitching' major policies like immigration to such an institution, there is need for great attention to be paid to whether the gender injustices associated with that institution can be alleviated. If they cannot be, is the dependence of immigration policy on marriage justifiable?

Having noted one major issue requiring careful conceptual examination, we wish to show examples of how detailed monitoring of particular policy provisions and practices can reveal that diverse groups of women and men may be specifically disadvantaged. This is not something that can readily be known from a general review of immigration policy and its history, and really requires the practical knowledge of an immigration officer to show how things work in practice. The two scenarios that follow are presented, then, for two reasons: first, to indicate how detailed must be the examination of particular policies and procedures if gender equity is to prevail in their implementation; and second, to emphasise that immigrant women and men are not homogeneous groups, for they differ on a host of dimensions like class, occupation/education and age in ways that can matter greatly for the advantage or disadvantage they experience from particular policies.

Scenario 1

An *Assurance of Support* is a document lodged with the DSS by an Australian resident or citizen sponsoring a person to immigrate to Australia. A sponsor is usually a relative, but it could be an employer lodging an Assurance of Support for an employee. The Assurance of Support covers a two-year period during which time, if the sponsored immigrant receives Unemployment Benefits (now Jobsearch Allowance), Sickness Allowance or Special Benefit, the cost is accrued by the sponsor as a debt to the Commonwealth and has to be repaid.

As of 1992, however, some sponsors have to lodge a bond as well, in the amount of $3500 for the principal person being sponsored and $1500 each for that person's dependants. An Assurance of Support (as of 1993) is a mandatory requirement for the following sponsored persons: Family entrants: parents, aged dependent relatives, orphan relatives, special need relatives, last remaining relatives and Lebanese concessional family entrants. Assurance of Support is not mandatory (and therefore no bond is attached) but can be requested by an immigration officer for a range of other classes of visa or entry permit, including spouse, dependent child and business classes.

How does this affect women, and in particular women of diverse characteristics? Assurances of Support are not usually accepted by the DSS from sponsors on pensions because of those sponsors' inability to repay debts. Similarly, a pension recipient might have difficulty finding $3500 for a bond. This particularly affects women on supporting parents' benefits, who may be sponsoring spouses.

Special-need relatives are sponsored by close relatives in Australia because those Australian relatives need assistance due to death, illness or serious disability, and they are in circumstances where there are too few services provided and no other relative able or willing to assist them is already here in Australia. Most commonly those who qualify as special-need relatives are daughters who will be carers for aged and invalid parents. Such parents would have to find $3500 to lodge as a bond for the daughter, plus an additional $1500 for her husband and each of her children if she should have any. There is a very strong probability that such parents are themselves pensioners and such a requirement might mean a great financial burden either on them or the daughter herself if she should provide the money. (According to the DSS, however, carers are entitled to a carer's

121

pension on becoming a resident without this affecting the Assurance of Support.)

Take, for a further example, the case where a woman, a single parent, has been retrenched and has sponsored her mother as a special-need relative to help look after her children while she searches for work. Under current arrangements, she would have to lodge a bond of $3500 for her mother. (See Immigration Review Tribunal (IRT) case no. 338 (IRT Research and Information Bulletin no. 10, 14 January 1992).) Other cases of special-need relatives are reported in IRT Research and Information Bulletins of 4 March 1991, 14 January 1992, 14 May 1991 and 11 June 1991. Note that these applications are all subject to a mandatory Assurance of Support, but were lodged before the introduction of the bond.

Scenario 2

In 1992, the *skills assessment* component of the Independent and Concessional Family categories of immigration would net an applicant up to 75 points of the 85 points then needed to enter Australia. For Independent category applicants other points were awarded for age—30 points under 30 years, 0 points over 50 years—and for language—15 points for English competence. Under the Concessional Family category, points for age were the same but instead of being assessed for English language ability, an applicant was awarded points for being sponsored by a relative (up to 15, depending on the relationship), for their sponsor being an Australian citizen (up to 10), for their sponsor being well settled (up to 10), and for their sponsor living in a designated area, usually non-metropolitan (5 points). This gives a possible total of 40 points.

Men are advantaged in the Skill component because, as we remarked earlier, of the masculine conceptualisation of skill in Australia. Applicants are assessed according to their 'usual occupation' and level of education and training. Occupations in Australia requiring formal qualifications such as a degree, diploma or trade certificate attract maximum points, depending on the level to which the applicant is qualified to pursue that occupation in Australia. Therefore the female-dominated sectors of the Australian labour market such as salespersons and clerical workers, not needing a certificate in Australia to work in those fields, attract no points for an applicant whose 'usual occupation' is in sales or clerical positions, that is, a large percentage of female applicants. (See IRT case no. 255 re Blay and IRT case no. 297 re Cho Cho Alice Wong in IRT Research and Information Bulletin no. 9, 14 January 1992.)

In assessing the points to be allocated for skill under either the Independent or the Concessional Family categories, the immigration officer has to consider the applicant's 'usual occupation', which is defined in the regulations as 'an occupation that the applicant has engaged in for gain or reward for a continuous period of at least six months during the period of two years immediately preceding the relevant application for a visa or entry permit'. Obviously women who have left the work force for child-bearing or child-care responsibilities could be regarded by immigration officers as not having a 'usual occupation' and therefore would be awarded no points for skill. Furthermore, the skills associated with domestic and child-care duties, to be valued as one's occupation, must be entered into for 'gain or reward'; therefore people engaged in unpaid domestic labour are considered not to have a 'usual occupation'.

The following cases from the IRT Research and Information Bulletin demonstrate this: case no. 111 re Ho, and case no. 115 re Lai Har Wong in Bulletin no. 5, 14 May 1991; case no. 157 re Desta Noelle Hall, Bulletin no. 7, 8 October 1991; case no. 333 re Casanada, Bulletin no. 10, 14 January 1992; also see case no. 72 re De Goederen.

Though immigration policies and practices are, indeed, far more gender-neutral than they were several decades ago, we believe that they can still be improved in the levels of gender equity they achieve for potential immigrants and for settlers already arrived. Both outcomes and processes can be bettered, but the process of thinking through how this can be achieved is difficult, given both the embeddedness of immigration selection in broader societal institutions like marital relationships or the masculinist definition of work-related skills, and the fact that the most obvious inequities for women in the immigration process have perhaps already been identified and alleviated. If criteria about gender equity and the acknowledgment of difference are used to inform scrutiny of what we now have and how that can be improved, however, some new policy angles can be identified. This concluding chapter has tried to suggest some of these.

Notes

Chapter 1: Gender equity and the analysis of immigration and settlement

1 Note that the Federal Government department responsible for immigration has undergone a series of name changes since 1947. The term Department of Immigration will be used in a generic sense. Where appropriate the specific title will be used, for example, Department of Immigration, Ethnic Affairs and Local Government (1987–early 1993).

Chapter 4: The state's influence on settlement prospects for immigrant women—the labour market and the 'double burden'

2 The labour force participation rate is the number of persons who are in the labour force expressed as a percentage of the total population (excluding the military and the institutionalised) aged 15 years and above in the same group (ABS 1991b, p. 24). This can be calculated for any group or for the population as a whole.

3 They were born in different countries and reflect different ethnicities. Most are from more recently established ethnic communities: five from Asian countries, two from Europe, one from South America and one from the Middle East. Four are from Third World countries, three from developing countries and two from developed countries. All had some post-secondary school education, are middle class, fluent English speakers and very articulate. One had been born in Australia of NESB parents, four others had been here a very long time and the remainder had been in Australia ten years or more.

References

Akcehk, R. & Elley, J. (eds) 1988, *Turkish Community in Australia*, Turkish-Australian Friendship Society, Melbourne.

Alcorso, C. 1991, 'Non-English speaking background women in the workforce', The Office of Multicultural Affairs, *Working Papers on Multiculturalism*, no. 4, Centre for Multicultural Studies, University of Wollongong, NSW.

Alcorso, C. & Harrison, G. 1991, *NESB Immigrant Women in the Australian Labour Force: Main Trends*, Preliminary Draft of a Report to the Commonwealth-State Council on Non-English Speaking Background Women's Issues, Canberra.

Anthias, F. 1983, 'Sexual divisions and ethnic adaptation: The case of Greek-Cypriot Women', in *One Way Ticket: Immigration and Female Labour*, ed. A. Phizacklea, Routledge & Kegan Paul, Melbourne.

Australian Bureau of Statistics (ABS) 1991a, *1990 Marriages Australia*, Commonwealth of Australia.

—— 1991b, *The Labour Market and Employment Characteristics of Immigrant Women in Australia*, AGPS, Canberra.

Australian Council of Social Service (ACOSS) 1992, *Draft Report of Study of the Role of Residential Location and Mobility in the Settlement Process*, BIR, Canberra.

Australian Council of Trade Unions (ACTU) 1991, ACTU Congress decision: Immigration and settlement 1991, Developments in Migration No. 74, Melbourne, ACTU, mimeo.

Barsotti, O. & Lecchini, L. 1991, 'The case of Asian female migrants', *Asian Migrant*, vol. IV, no. 2, April-June.

Bennett, L. 1984, 'The construction of skill: craft unions, women workers and the Conciliation and Arbitration Court', *Law in Context*, vol. 2, pp. 118-32.

Bertone, S. & Griffin, G. 1992, *Immigrant Workers and Trade Unions*, AGPS, Canberra.

Birrell, R. 1990, *The Chains that Bind: Family Reunion Migration*, AGPS, Canberra.

Bittman, M. 1991, *Juggling Time: How Australian Families Use Time*, AGPS, Canberra.

Borowski, A. & Shu, J. 1992, *Australia's Population Trends and Prospects 1991*, AGPS, Canberra.

Bottomley, G. 1984, 'Women on the move: Migration and feminism', in *Ethnicity, Class and Gender in Australia*, eds G. Bottomley & M. de Lepervanche, Allen & Unwin, Sydney.

Boyd, M. 1986, 'Immigrant women in Canada', in *International Migration: the Female Experience*, eds R. J. Simon & C. B. Brettell, Rowman & Allenheld, Totawa, NJ.

—— 1987, *Migrant Women in Canada: Profiles and Policies*, Immigration Research Working Paper no. 2, Employment and Immigration Canada, Ottawa.

Boyd, M., Mulvihill, M. A. & Myles, J. 1991, 'Gender, power and postindustrialism', *The Canadian Review of Sociology and Anthropology*, vol. 28, no. 4, pp. 407-36.

Boyd, M. & Taylor, C. 1986, 'The feminization of temporary workers: the Canadian case', *Quarterly Review of the Intergovernmental Committee for Migration*, OECD, vol. XXIV, no. 4.

Bureau of Immigration Research (BIR) 1991, *Immigration Update: December Quarter 1990*, AGPS, Canberra.

Burnley, I. H. 1974, 'International migration and metropolitan growth in Australia', in *Urbanization in Australia*, ed. I. H. Burnley, Cambridge University Press, London.

—— 1985, 'Cities of immigrants: migration, growth and heterogeneity' in *Living in Cities*, eds I. Burnley & J. Forrest, Allen & Unwin, Sydney.

Cahill, D. 1990, *Intermarriages in International Context: A Study of Filipino Women Married to Australian, Japanese and Swiss Men*, Scalabrini Migration Center, Quezon City, Philippines.

Campbell, I., Fincher, R., Webber, M. 1991, 'Occupational mobility in segmented labour markets: the experience of immigrant workers in Melbourne', *Australian and New Zealand Journal of Sociology*, vol. 27, no. 2, pp. 172-94.

Carmichael, G. A. 1988, *With This Ring: First Marriage Patterns, Trends and Prospects in Australia*, ANU & Australian Institute of Family Studies, Canberra.

Chafetz, J. S. 1990, *Gender Equity*, Sage, Newbury Park, Calif.

Chuah, F., Chuah, L. D., Reid-Smith, L., Rice, A. & Rowley, K. 1987, 'Does Australia have a Filipina brides problem?', *Australian Journal of Social Issues*, vol. 22, no. 4.

Cohen, L. M. 1977, 'The female factor in resettlement', *Society*, pp. 27-30.

Collins, J. 1988, *Migrant Hands in A Distant Land*, Pluto Press, Sydney.

Conybeare, C. 1992, Closing address, Presented at the Bureau of Immigration Research Women in Migration Conference, Melbourne, mimeo.

Cruz, V. & Paganoni, A. 1989, *Filipinas in Migration: Big Bills and Small Change*, Scalabrini Migration Center, Quezon City, Philippines.

Davis, B. 1988, 'Fraud and annulment of marriage', *Australian Journal of Family Law*, vol. 2, no. 2, pp. 138-63.

Dawkins, P., Lewis, P., Norris, K., Baker, M., Robertson, F., Groenewold, N. & Hagger, A. 1991, *Flows of Immigrants to South Australia, Tasmania and Western Australia*, AGPS, Canberra.

de Lepervanche, M. 1989 'Breeders for Australia: A national identity for women?', *Australian Journal of Social Issues*, vol. 24, no. 3, pp. 163-82.

Department of Employment, Education and Training (DEET) 1990, *Women and Work*, Women's Bureau, vol. 12, nos. 2, 3, Canberra.

Department of Immigration and Ethnic Affairs (or Local Government and Ethnic Affairs) 1959, 1964, 1971, 1972, 1976, 1982, 1989, *Procedures Advice Manuals* and *Migrant Entry Handbooks*, Department of Immigration, Canberra.

Department of Immigration 1971, *Facts and Figures About Immigration*, Canberra.

Department of Immigration Files: 63/46044, 65/46611, 67/70369, 69/70582, 69/71003, 69/72632, 69/72633, 69/72663, 72/77443, 72/76644, 74/77192, 74/77682, 76/76327, 83/76479, 89/30296, A90/11114.

Department of Immigration and Ethnic Affairs (DIEA) 1981, *Migrant Women in Australia: The Settlement Experience*, DIEA, Canberra.

—— 1982a, *A Bride for All Reasons: Report on a Pilot Survey of Filipino Brides*, DIEA, Melbourne.

—— 1982b, *Migrant Entry Handbook*, AGPS, Canberra.

Department of Immigration, Local Government and Ethnic Affairs (DILGEA) 1989a, *Migrant Entry Handbook*, AGPS, Canberra.

—— 1989b, *Procedures Advice Manual De Facto Marriage Relationships*, AGPS, Canberra.

—— 1989c, *Procedures Advice Manual Marriage and Divorce*, AGPS, Canberra.

—— 1989d, *Procedures Advice Manual Permanent Entry Visas 3: Spouse—(Class 100)*, AGPS, Canberra.

—— 1990a, *Procedures Advice Manual Conditional Visas and Entry Permits 3: Prospective Marriage (Class 300)*, 3rd edn, AGPS, Canberra.

—— 1990b, *Procedures Advice Manual Family Unit and Dependency*, 3rd edn, AGPS, Canberra.

—— 1990c, *Procedures Advice Manual*, AGPS, Canberra.

—— 1991a, *AMEP National Plan 1991–1992*, DILGEA, Canberra.

—— 1991b, *Corporate Plan 1991–93*, DILGEA, Canberra.

—— 1991c, Migration Regulations (Amendment), *Folk Law*, vol. 3, no. 5.

—— 1991d, *Women's Issues Plan*, AGPS, Canberra.

—— 1991e, *Tougher Rules for Temporary Entrants in Marriage or De Facto Relationships*, Media release MPS 4/91, Canberra.

—— 1991f, *New Immigration Arrangements for Temporary Entrants in Marriages or De Facto Relationships begin Monday*, Media release MPS 23/91, Canberra.

—— 1991g, *Migration Regulations: Unofficial Consolidation as at 5 July 1991*, AGPS, Canberra.

—— 1991h, *Review '91 Annual Report 1990–91*, AGPS, Canberra.

—— 1992a, *Residence Sub-Program Historical Summary*, Resident Status Data, Canberra.

—— 1992b, *Staff News*, issue no. 584, 27 March, pp. 6–7.

—— 1992c, *Review '92 Annual Report 1991–92*, AGPS, Canberra.

D'Mello, A. 1990, 'Child care access: a matter of culture', *Migration Action*, vol. XII, no. 2, p. 3.

Easteal, P. 1992, *The Forgotten Few: Overseas-Born Women in Australian Prisons*, AGPS, Canberra.

Eliadis, M., Colanero, R. & Roussos, P. (n.d.), *Issues for Non-English Speaking Background Women in Multicultural Australia*, Office of Multicultural Affairs, Canberra.

Elley, J. 1985, 'Party selling: a new form of traditional hospitality amongst Turkish women migrants in Melbourne', in *Australian Ways: Anthropological Studies of an Industrialised Society*, ed. L. Manderson, Allen & Unwin, Sydney.

—— 1988, 'Calisan hanimlar: Turkish migrant women at work', in *Turkish Community in Australia*, eds R. Akcelik & J. Elley, Australian-Turkish Friendship Society Publications, Melbourne.

Fawcett, J. T., Khoo, S. E. & Smith, P. C. (eds) 1984, *Women in the Cities of Asia: Migration and Urban Adaptation*, Westview Press Inc., USA.

Fincher, R. 1991, *Immigration, Urban Infrastructure and the Environment*, AGPS, Canberra.

Fincher, R., Campbell, I. & Webber, M. 1993, 'Multiculturalism, settlement and migrants' income and employment strategies', in *Multiculturalism, Difference and Postmodernism*, eds G. Clark, D. Forbes & R. Francis, Longman Cheshire, Melbourne.

Fincher, R., Foster, L., Giles, W. & Preston, V. (forthcoming), 'Gender in Migration', in *Immigration and Refugee Policy: Australia and Canada Compared*, eds H. Adelman, A. Borowski, M. Burstein & L. Foster, Melbourne University Press, Melbourne.

Foster, L., Marshall, A. & Williams, L. 1991, *Discrimination Against Immigrant Workers in Australia*, AGPS, Canberra.

Foster, L. & Rado, M. 1991, *Literacy Needs of Non-English Speaking Background Women*, Division of Further Education, Ministry of Education, Melbourne.

Gibson, K. & Graham J. 1986, 'Situating migrants in theory: the case of Filipino migrant contract construction workers', *Capital and Class*, no. 29, pp. 130–47.

Glenn, E. N. 1986, *Issei, Nisei, War Brides*, Temple University Press, Philadelphia.

Gray, I., Dunn, P., Kelly, B. & Williams, C. 1991, *Immigrant Settlement in Country Areas*, AGPS, Canberra.

Grossman, J. 1984, 'The occupational attainment of immigrant women in Sweden', *Scandinavian Journal of Economics*, vol. 86, no. 3, pp. 337-51.

Hartman, H. & Hartman, M. 1983, 'The effect of immigration on women's roles in various countries', *International Journal of Sociology and Social Policy*, vol. 3, no. 3, pp. 86-103.

Hassan, R., Healy, J. & McKenna, R. 1985, 'Lebanese Families', in *Ethnic Family Values in Australia*, editor-in-chief D. Storer, Prentice-Hall, Sydney.

Horvath, R. & Engels, B. 1985, 'The residential restructuring of inner Sydney', in *Living in Cities*, eds I. H. Burnley & J. Forrest, Allen & Unwin, Sydney.

Hugo, G. 1990, 'Demographic and spatial aspects of immigration', in *Australian Immigration: A Survey of the Issues*, eds M. Wooden, R. Holton, G. Hugo & J. Sloan, AGPS, Canberra, pp. 24-109.

Immigration Review Tribunal (IRT) 'Cases', in *Folk Law*, vol. 3, no. 3, May 1991; vol. 3, no. 5, September 1991; IRT Research and Information Bulletin, nos 3 and 4, March 1991; no. 5, May 1991; no. 6, June 1991; nos 7 and 8, October 1991; no. 10, January 1992.

Jackson, R. & Flores, E. 1989, *No Filipinos in Manila: A Study of Filipino Migrants in Australia*, James Cook University, Townsville.

Jaggar, A. 1991, 'Feminist ethics: projects, problems, prospects', in *Feminist Ethics*, ed. C. Card, University of Kansas Press, Lawrence, Kansas.

Jakubowicz, A., Morrissey, M. & Palser, J. 1984, *Ethnicity, Class and Social Policy in Australia*, Social Welfare Research Centre, University of New South Wales, SWRC Reports and Proceedings no. 46.

Joint Standing Committee on Migration Regulations (JSCMR) 1991, *Change of Status: Marriage and De Facto Relationships*, Second report, Parliament of the Commonwealth of Australia, AGPS, Canberra.

Jupp, J., McRobbie, A. & York, B. 1991, *Settlement Needs of Small Newly Arrived Ethnic Groups*, AGPS, Canberra.

Knowles, J. 1985, Vietnamese refugee women and employment, Perth, Western Australia, 1978-1984, Paper presented at the Women in Asia Workshop, Australian National University, Canberra, 11-13 July.

Kunek, S. 1988, *Women of the Mediterranean*, Greek-Australian Workshops, Centre for Migrant and Intercultural Studies, Monash University, Clayton.

—— 1989, 'Greek female migration in the post World War II period in Australia', *Australian Studies*, no. 2, pp. 36-58.

Lam, T. C., Luong, T. L. & Cahill, D. 1989, 'Vietnamese female outworkers in Melbourne's western suburbs', *Asian Migrant II*, vol. 2, no. 3, pp. 95-8.

Leeds, A. 1976, 'Women in the migratory process: a reductionist outlook', *Anthropological Quarterly*, no. 49, pp. 69-76.

Lever-Tracy, C. & Ip, D. 1992, Asian women in business, Bureau of Immigration Research, Melbourne, mimeo.

Lie, S. 1983, *Immigrant Women in Norway*, International Affairs Monograph Series, Asian Research Service, Hong Kong.

Lycklama, G. 1989, 'Trade in maids: Asian domestic helpers in migration theory and practice', in *The Trade in Domestic Helpers*, Asian and Pacific Development Centre, Kuala Lumpur.

Lynch, P. 1970, *The Woman's Role in Immigration*, Address to the National Immigration Committee of the YWCA, Melbourne, 2 May.

McCallum, J. & Gelfand, D. 1990, *Ethnic Women in the Middle: A Focus Group Study of Daughters Caring for Older Migrants in Australia*, National Centre for Epidemiology and Population Health, Australian National University, Canberra.

Madden, R. & Young, S. 1993a, Transcripts of consultations for women and men immigrating to Australia: their characteristics and immigration decisions, Bureau of Immigration Research, Melbourne, mimeo.

—— 1993b, *Women and Men Immigrating to Australia: Their Characteristics and Immigration Decisions*, AGPS, Canberra.

Mageean, P. 1990, *Pathways to participation: the vocational and further education needs of adult immigrants in rural Australia*, TAFE National Centre for Research and Development, Leabrook, SA.

Manderson, L. & Inglis, C. 1984, 'Turkish migration and workforce participation in Sydney, Australia', *International Migration Review*, vol. 18, no. 2, pp. 258-75.

Martin, H. 1989, *Angels and Arrogant Gods: Migration Officers and Migrants Reminisce 1945-85*, Canberra, AGPS.

Martin, J. 1984, 'Non-English-speaking women: production and social reproduction', in *Ethnicity, Class and Gender in Australia*, eds G. Bottomley & M. de Lepervanche, Allen & Unwin, Sydney.

—— 1991, 'Multiculturalism and feminism', in *Intersexions*, eds G. Bottomley, M. de Lepervanche & J. Martin, Allen & Unwin, Sydney.

Migrant Women's Working Centre 1991, Background paper for National Conference on Migrant Women, Settlement and Training, Adelaide, May, mimeo.

Miltenyi, G, 1988, Trade Unions in a Multicultural Workforce, Office of Multicultural Affairs, Canberra, mimeo.

Misztal, B. 1991, 'Migrant women in Australia', *Policy Organisation and Society*, no. 3, Winter, pp. 50-61.

Mitchell, C., Tait, D. & Castles, S. 1990, *The Recognition of Overseas Professional Qualifications*, AGPS, Canberra.

Morokvasic, M. 1981, 'The invisible ones: A double role of women in the current European migrations', in *Strangers in the World*, eds L. Eitinger & D. Schwartz, Hans Huber, Bern, Stuttgart, Vienna.

—— 1983, 'Women in migration: Beyond the reductionist outlook', in *One Way ticket: Migration and Female Labour*, ed. A. Phizacklea, Routledge & Kegan Paul, Melbourne.

—— 1991, 'Roads to independence. Self-employed immigrants and minority women in five European States', *International Migration Review*, vol. XXIX, no. 3, pp. 407-20.

Mottee, M. 1992, Immigrant women and domestic violence, Paper presented at the Bureau of Immigration Research, Women in Migration Conference, Melbourne, mimeo.

National Population Council, Population Issues Committee 1992, *Population Issues and Australia's Future. Final Report*, AGPS, Canberra.

Neuman, N. & Elder, K. 1982, 'Migrant women outworkers in Australia', *Refractory Girl*, no. 23, pp. 6-8.

New South Wales Department of Industrial Relations and Employment, Women's Directorate 1987, *Self-Employed or Employee?: A Survey of Women in New South Wales Doing Paid Work at Home*, Sydney.

Ng, R. 1988, *The Politics of Community Services*, Garamond Press, Toronto.

Nicolaou, L. 1991, *Australian Unions and Immigrant Workers*, Allen & Unwin, Sydney.

Pendlebury, J. 1990, *Filipino Brides in Remote Areas*, Occasional paper no. 5, North Australia Development Unit of the Department of Social Security, Darwin, NT.

Pettman, J. 1992, *Living in the Margins*, Allen & Unwin, Sydney.

Phizacklea, A. 1983, *One Way Ticket: Migration and Female Labour,* Routledge & Kegan Paul, Melbourne.

Pohjola, A. 1991 'Social networks—help or hindrance to the migrant?', *International Migration*, vol. XXIX, no. 3, pp. 435-43.

Public Service Commission (PSC) 1990, *Maximising Diversity*, APGS, Canberra.

Radcliffe, S. 1990, 'Ethnicity, patriarchy, and incorporation into the nation: female migrants as domestic servants in Peru', *Environment and Planning D: Society and Space*, no. 8, pp. 379-93.

Rayner, M. 1992, 'Working in the new country: migrant women and discrimination', *BIR Bulletin*, number six, April, pp. 34-6.

Rush, J. & Steen, F. 1987, *'And . . . Giving Our Lives To This Country': A Summary Report of Spanish-Speaking Women in the Workforce*, AGPS, Canberra.

Seitz, A. & Kilmartin, C. 1987, *'Don't Assume the Stereotype': A pilot study of women of non-English speaking background in Melbourne*, DIEA, Victoria.

Simon, R. & Bretell, C. B. (eds) 1986, *International Migration: The Female Experience*, Rowman & Allenheld, Totawa, NJ.

Smith, M. E. 1980, 'The Portuguese female immigrant: The "marginal man"', *International Migration Review*, vol. 14, no. 1, pp. 77–92.

Snedden, B. 1968, *The Migrant and Human Rights*, Good Neighbour Council of Victoria, Melbourne.

Storer, D. 1976, *'But I wouldn't want my wife to work here . . .': A Study of Migrant Women in Melbourne Industry*, Centre for Urban Research and Action, Fitzroy, Victoria.

Tait, D. & Gibson, K. 1987, 'Economic and ethnic restructuring: an analysis of migrant labour in Sydney', *Journal of Intercultural Studies*, no. 8, pp. 1–26.

Thadani, V. N. & Todaro, M. P. 1978, *Toward a Theory of Female Migration in Developing Countries*, Centre for Policy Studies, Population Council, New York.

Tienda, M. & Booth, K. 1991, 'Gender, migration and social change', *International Sociology*, vol. 6, no. 1, pp. 51–72.

Tienda, M., Jensen, L. & Bach, R. 1984, 'Immigration, gender and the process of occupational change in the United States, 1970-80', *International Migration Review*, vol. xviii, no. 4, pp. 1021–44.

Vasta, E. 1985, *If you had your time again, would you migrate to Australia?': A Study of Long-Settled Italo-Australians in Brisbane*, AGPS, Canberra.

Victorian Department of Labour 1989, *Child Care in Victoria and Women's Access to the Labour Market*, Labour Market Research and Policy Branch, Working paper no. 22, Melbourne.

Victorian Trades Hall Council 1991, *Facing the Challenge: Women in Victorian Unions*, VTHC, Melbourne.

Webber, M. 1991, 'Settlement characteristics of immigrants to Australia', in *Countries of Immigrants*, eds G. Freeman & J. Jupp, Oxford University Press, Sydney.

Webber, M., Campbell, I. & Fincher, R. 1990, 'Ethnicity, gender and industrial restructuring in Australia, 1971-1986', *Journal of Intercultural Studies*, vol. 11, no. 1, pp. 1–48.

Wellesley Editorial Committee 1977, *Women and National Development: The Complexities of Change*, University of Chicago Press, Chicago and London.

Women's Ethnic Network (WEN) Vic. 1990, *Fish Out of Water*, Report of the WEN Access and Advocacy Project, Melbourne.

Wong, M. & Hirschman, C. 1983, 'Labor force participation and socioeconomic attainment of Asian–American women', *Sociological Perspectives*, vol. 26, no. 4, pp. 423–46.

Woo, D. 1985, 'The socioeconomic status of Asian American women in the labor force', *Sociological Perspectives*, vol. 28, no. 3, pp. 307–38.

Wooden, M., Holton, R., Hugo, G. & Sloan, J. 1990, *Australian Immigration: A Survey of the Issues*, AGPS, Canberra.

Yeatman, A. 1988, *A Review of Multicultural Policies and Programs in Children's Services with Particular Emphasis on Childcare Services*, Office of Multicultural Affairs, Sydney.

Young, I. M. 1990, *Justice and the Politics of Difference*, Princeton University Press, Princeton.

Index